Writing to Please Your Boss

T5-DHD-070

Demo Copy
Resale Prohibited

Demo Copy
Resale Prohibited

Writing to Please Your Boss

& Other Important People
Including Yourself

- Reports
- Proposals,
- Feasibility Studies
- Memoranda

   on Time and on Target

Demo Copy
Resale Prohibited

Elizabeth Cohn and Susan Kleimann

PC
PRESS

© Copyright 1989, P.C. Press. All rights reserved.
Except for the inclusion of brief quotations in a review, no part of this book
may be reproduced or used in any form or by any means, electronic or
mechanical, including photocopying, recording, or by any information storage
and retrieval system, without permission in writing from the publisher.

P.C. PRESS
51 Monroe St., Suite 1101, Rockville, MD 20850

Distributed by
ACROPOLIS BOOKS LTD., Washington, D.C. 20009

Library of Congress Cataloging-in-Publication Data

Cohn, Elizabeth, 1949-
   Writing to please your boss and other important people including yourself.

   1. Business report writing. I. Kleimann, Susan, 1946-   . II. Title.
HF5719.C64   1989   808.06665   89-18518
ISBN 1-878322-04-4

"Post-it" is a trademark of 3M. IBM is a registered trademark of International
Business Machines Corporation.

C O N T E N T S

Demo Copy
Resale Prohibited

ACKNOWLEDGMENTS

We wish to thank Steve Frankel of Scandinavian PC Systems, who served as instigator, impresario and general editor of this book. We particularly wish to thank him for his contribution of Chapter 8, "Computers Can Help." We are indebted to Jean Bernard, who edited several drafts of the book, for her keen eye and good humor, and to Joanne Frankel, for the title. Kathy Karlson has provided us with intelligent and insightful conversations about many of our central concepts.

We are also indebted to Bob Kleimann for his unflagging devotion to keeping our computer running and producing copy (often through the night), and for his frequent and helpful interventions and solutions. We thank Rachel Cohn for her editorial assistance, Kristin Kleimann for her sense of design and the painstaking copying of answers onto worksheets, and David Kleimann for his suggestions of scenario details.

Several consultants and publishers have allowed us to reprint from their materials. We are grateful to Connie Drake Wilson, of Wilson Associates, for contributing material on graphics. We are grateful to W. W. Norton and Company, Inc. for permission to reprint "How to Lie with Statistics," by Darrell Huff and Irving Geis, and to The Guilford Press, for permission to quote from "Writing at Exxon ITD: Notes on the Writing Environment of an R & D Organization," by James Paradis, David Dobrin, and Richard Miller, which appeared in *Writing in Nonacademic Settings*.

We are grateful for the time and insight of Dr. Tad Pula, Advisory Engineer, Electronic Systems Group of Westinghouse Electric Corporation, who was kind enough to offer detailed comments on several of our drafts. We are indebted to Dorothy Strohecker, Robert Greene, Carolyn Hill, and Bob Slevin, who also offered valuable comments on drafts. And we appreciate the support and encouragement of our friends and clients, particularly Planning Research Corporation of McLean, Virginia, for whose training program we originally developed many of the concepts in this book.

Finally, we thank our many students and seminar participants who helped us clarify our own thinking, challenged us to think of even better ways to present our ideas, and ultimately provided us with assurance and proof that our methods do help.

Elizabeth Cohn is Vice President of Braestrup, Cohn and Associates, a training and educational consulting group. She specializes in methods of managing the planning process for large projects. She has extensive training experience with government agencies, international organizations, and private industry, and has conducted courses across the United States and abroad. She is a former member of the English Department at Georgetown University in Washington, D.C., and has also served as Assistant Director of Freshman English at the University of Maryland, College Park.

Susan Kleimann is a writing consultant with extensive training experience in government agencies and private industry. She has conducted courses throughout the United States and abroad. She specializes in the issues that surround the review process in large organizations, and has recently completed a two-year study of the review process for a federal agency. She has also taught at the University of Maryland, Prince George's Community College, and Anne Arundel Community College. Her dissertation for the Ph.D. in English deals with the problems of corporate writing.

Everybody—just about—has a boss. But everybody wants to be in charge. How can you be in charge of your own writing and still please your boss? The answer lies, very often, in helping your boss communicate with you. You can learn to work with your boss to articulate what he or she wants, and why—and you can get your boss to sign off on your work before you ever draft it. How? You can use the Decision Method to identify the real decisions you must make for any writing project you do on the job.

Writing to Please Your Boss takes you through the Decision Method, a series of decisions you can make to fulfill any writing assignment. The decisions allow you to plan your work more explicitly and to collaborate more directly with managers and colleagues as the work progresses. And because you, as a busy professional, will rarely be able to clear whole days at a time for writing, this book will show you how to divide the decision process into ninety-minute modules. The result? You will use this book to make efficient use of the time available—for effective, sophisticated results even when you're writing under pressure.

The Decision Method will help you prevent surprises: surprises for your boss (who didn't at all have in mind what you wrote,) and surprises for you (when the work comes back to be redone). The Decision Method will help you collaborate—with your boss or work team—to make writing decisions and share the results at key points.

Writing to Please Your Boss treats writing as a fact of professional life. Whether you work for General Motors, the Red Cross, or a government agency, your organization has a tremendous impact on your writing. This book shows you how to apply systematic thinking to writing problems you encounter in the workplace. The techniques demonstrated in this book can work either for individual writers or for teams of writers, and they apply to the kind of collaborative writing that many large projects require. They can save you time, money, and morale. Since our approach is a "how to" approach, use this book to work through a current project of your own—a report or proposal—from start to finish. Apply each decision as you come to it. Like the participants in our workplace seminars, you, too, will use the Decision Method to gain a greater sense of control over your writing.

Will you experience an overnight transformation in your writing? Not likely. But you will procrastinate less and meet deadlines more easily. You'll be able to predict more realistic timeframes and designate writing tasks, because you'll know what tasks are involved. You'll be better able to focus the attention of reviewers, because your drafts will be clearer. Under normal circumstances, you'll find your reports processed more quickly. And you will gain greater confidence.

Writing is a complex activity; it will still be work. But this book can help you make writing work better for you.

CHAPTER ONE

The Writing Process

The Individual Writer

Writing is a high-risk activity. To some people, writing feels like jumping off the Empire State Building—naked. They feel exposed and threatened when they have to put something in writing. Even if writing involves no such dramatic feelings for you, you may experience it as a struggle. (Chances are good that you do—otherwise, why did you pick up this book?) If you are writing in an organization, as part of your job, your struggles to write may be multiplied by other professional struggles.

In this chapter, we'll be talking about individual writers, working in an organizational environment—and sometimes bucking the current. We'll consider what happens when an individual writes, and how the individual's preferences affect his or her work in an organization. We'll look at writing in two ways: first, as a process, and second, as a series of decisions.

Writing as a Process

First let's consider writing as a process. Writing tends to be recursive—you cycle through phases of the process over and over, until you get what you want. But if you are going to schedule milestones or meet a deadline, you need to make linear distinctions in the process. To work in a corporate setting, you need to be able to make rough predictions about where you'll be in the process when.

A simple linear way of defining the process is to give it three phases: **plan, draft, revise.** Consider your own preferences in this process. Left entirely to yourself to do a writing project, how do you tend to work? Suppose someone gave you ten units worth of resources—time and energy—how would you tend to invest them in the three phases of the writing process? Take a moment to distribute the ten units on the chart below. (Be sure to answer the question in terms of what you actually do, rather than what you think you should do.)

Plan	+ Draft	+ Revise	= Total Units
			10

Your Comfort Pattern

What kind of distribution did you come up with? Do you have a fairly even distribution, or do you tend to have all your eggs in one basket?

If you're like most people, right now you're probably expecting us to spring a so-called right answer on you for this exercise. We're not really going to do that. Most distributions (with the exception of all ten units in Plan, or all ten in Revise) are capable of yielding a satisfactory product—when it's entirely up to you to develop the product. That is, the distribution is just one way of starting to look at your individual preferences as a writer: **your comfort pattern.**

Comfort patterns tend to vary according to the writing environment. For instance, you might find it interesting to know that many literary writers rely heavily on the revising phase. (Mark Twain made himself popular with his publisher by completely revising one of his books in the galley-proofs, the final stage before publication.) Literary writers may be, of all writers, the most likely to insist on rewriting and rewriting. We picture them laboring to get just the right word, the exact nuance.

Newspaper reporters, on the other hand, may have little time available for revising—and planning for most news stories is provided by the reporter's "who-what-when-where-how" system. In the newspaper environment, writers may rely heavily on the drafting phase of the process. Newswriters, in fact, may be the most likely of all writers to get away with just sitting down at the word processor and composing.

Writing in an Organization

In the writing environment of an organization, however, you need to rely on the planning process. So what happened to our promise of no right answer? We still hold to that promise: no single answer is right for the individual writer, working autonomously. But here's the problem: in an organization, almost no one writes autonomously. You generally are collaborating with colleagues, delegating work to subordinates, or being reviewed by managers above you in the corporate hierarchy.

We can say several things about writing in an organization. For one thing, it tends to be highly collaborative, as in, for instance, proposal writing and the review process. For another thing, it may involve complex information, as in developing technical manuals. And, finally, it often requires extensive analysis on the part of the writer, as in feasibility studies. When any one of these factors is present in a writing project, you will be most productive when you engage in systematic planning.

But, you may protest, your writing environment is often like the newspaper reporter's: you write under deadline. True. As we acknowledged up front, pressure is a fact of life for most professionals. But the demands you face may well be different from the demands the reporter faces. On the one hand, the reporter knows the newspaper's audience, and can rely on it to remain the same from day to day. You, on the other hand, may not have that same luxury. Your audience may well vary. You may sometimes be writing for readers who know little or nothing about your area, or for potential clients who have to be convinced that you know what you're talking about. In short, you may need a more elaborate decision-making process for writing than does the reporter.

The rest of this chapter will help you understand writing as a decision-making process, so that you can engage in effective—and efficient—planning, drafting, and revising in your writing projects. We'll look next at the Decision Cycle for writing, and then match it to your comfort pattern. Finally, we'll consider the Decision Cycle in terms of the comfort pattern for most organizations.

Elements of the Process

What goes into the hopper when you write? That is, what are some of the elements you feel you have to deal with—what's on your mind when you write? Take sixty seconds to brainstorm what goes into the hopper.

What did you come up with? Facts, details, ideas, structure, readers, punctuation, grammar, clerical support, deadlines, formats . . . you may have some of these, all of these, or many more than these. Dozens of possibilities exist, and they represent quite a handful of things to deal with. Some are more subject to your control than others. You need to simplify the number and gain greater control over the most crucial ones.

The Decision Cycle

Four elements always affect the quality of the final product, and consequently must be dealt with in the process. They are **situation, facts, concepts,** and **structure**, and are illustrated below. Although various constraints, like time or pressure, affect your project, these four elements help you counteract the negative effects of your constraints. We'll show how these four elements, taken together, constitute the Decision Cycle. Then, in the next chapter, we'll introduce our Fourteen Decisions for Writers, based on the cycle.

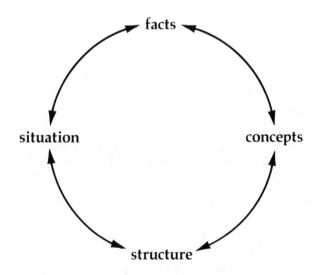

WRITING TO PLEASE YOUR BOSS

The Situation

The first element to consider is the situation in which the product will be used. In most organizations, situation drives the writing project. That is, your writing needs to be directed to a specific purpose and audience. You also need to clearly define your subject and what role you should play. The combination of these needs makes up the writing situation: purpose, audience, subject, and writer's role.

The Facts

The facts represent what you know about the subject: the data you have collected, the details of the matter. The facts are the specific pieces of information on which you base whatever analysis you will make. They are not themselves the analysis, and, for this reason, the facts don't speak for themselves. (Part of your mission in the decision-making process is to make them speak for you and to your audience.)

The Concepts

The concepts represent the basis on which you interpret the facts: the groupings, the relationships, the meanings you assign to the facts. These range from simple categorical groupings to theoretical assumptions. Facts and concepts combine to yield your analysis. (Later on, we'll talk about storyboarding as a way of establishing a viable interpretation of the facts.)

The Structure

Once you have interpreted the facts conceptually, you have something to say. You now need a structure to present your message. In planning a writing project, this element can be represented by an outline. (We'll discuss outlines in more detail later.) In the actual written product, structure is what the reader first perceives: an orderly progression of titles, captions, and paragraphs. In any event, structure is the element that gives form to the message, that allows you to present it logically.

What is structure based on? This question brings us back to situation. You need to plan a structure appropriate to your situation, one suitable for your purpose, audience, subject, and writer's role.

Message and Presentation

Now that you have the four elements of the Decision Cycle, you need to consider one additional aspect of it. You can divide the cycle itself into two halves: one half represents what you want to say, and the other half represents how you want to say it. That is, the combination of facts and concepts (your analysis) determines your **message.** The combination of situation and structure determines your **presentation**.

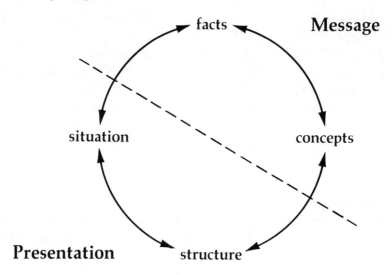

Short-Circuiting the Cycle

Be honest, now. Are you absolutely convinced that you need all of the elements of the Decision Cycle just named? Chances are that you had some reservations about the complete usefulness of at least one of them. If you did, you aren't different from most people. Most people have at least one blind spot on the cycle, an element they prefer not to give as much attention to. When this tendency is pronounced, it can result in genuine writer's block. At the very least, failure to cycle completely through every element results in frustration, incomplete work, and repeating the process later. In fact, we can say that learning to write efficiently might well be a process of learning to expose and deal with your weaknesses.

The Decision Cycle
and Your Comfort Pattern

In order to produce an effective product, you have to cycle completely through the Decision Cycle. But different writers move through the cycle at different paces. Go back and look at your comfort pattern. If you had most of your units in one column, very likely that means that you tend to cycle through the entire Decision Cycle in that phase (for instance, drafting) of the writing process. If you had your units evenly distributed, it means that you tend to distribute your writing decisions across the entire writing process.

The Decision Cycle
and the Organization's Comfort Pattern

Not only do comfort patterns vary according to the environment, they also tend to be highly individual. Following your comfort pattern when you are entirely responsible for a written product is generally productive, assuming that you cycle completely through the Decision Cycle. Unfortunately, as we also pointed out earlier, when you write in an organization, you will rarely write autonomously. When others are involved in a writing project, whether as co-drafters of the product, or as assignment-makers and reviewers, insisting on your own comfort pattern may prove counterproductive. You may need to adjust to the needs of the others involved in the project.

You might look at it this way: the organization has its own comfort pattern. Organizations are made up of people who have to work together in certain ways. For this reason, the requirements of other people involved in the project need to be considered. To accommodate everyone's share in the decision-making process, and to ensure that everyone has maximum input in the decisions, the decisions need to be made explicitly, and with minimum ego risk. For these reasons, the organization's comfort pattern requires an emphasis on the planning process.

Why Bother?

Put to the question, most people will at least give lip service to the value of planning. Put to the test, though, many people get rid of planning first. "Sure, it's a good idea to plan," they say. "But I don't have time."

Let's face it. You probably write under the gun fairly often. You send your work forward and it comes back—sometimes as if shot out of a cannon—to be reworked. This process also is a fact of corporate life. No wonder so many people find writing a challenge—the reward for writing under pressure often is *more* writing under pressure. But you can break out of this cycle by heeding this paradox: when you are *most* under pressure, you can *least* afford not to plan. Why? Because you can't afford to make mistakes—it has to hit the mark (or nearly hit it) the first time.

Remember, the organization has a comfort pattern too. And that pattern often involves a network of people working on a given project. Because this pattern represents the nature of writing in an organization, your decision-making pattern has to match other people's decision-making patterns: your boss's, and, if you're collaborating, your colleagues'. An explicit planning process, agreed upon by all involved, can help you match your process to the needs or demands of others working with you.

Even if your project is entirely self-initiated, you might want to consider another reason for explicit planning. Chances are that your work is complex, and you will be faced with keeping things straight in your head: facts, figures, opinions, analyses, and deadlines. But it's hard to keep a number of things in mind at once. Information theory tells us that the load most people can process is seven items (plus or minus two) at one time. You've already seen that a writing project requires you to handle a multitude of items. Now you need to break that multitude into manageable modules.

The Modules

A great deal of evidence suggests that the human body works in cycles of approximately ninety minutes. That's why people need breaks every so often to work effectively. You can get the most out of your working time by matching your work cycle to your body cycle. To make this match, distribute your writing tasks into modules that you can work on in ninety-minute blocks of time.

You can divide the decisions for a large project into four Decision Modules, which you can use to cycle several times through the Decision Cycle. Decision Module A takes you through the planning decisions for the **writing situation**; Decision Module B completes the planning decisions through the **facts**, **concepts**, and **structure** areas of the Decision Cycle. Decision Module C takes you all the way around the cycle again, as you draft the product you have planned in the two earlier modules. Decision Module D takes you once again around the cycle, as you rethink the product in the revising phase of the writing process.

You may need to apply more than one ninety-minute block of working time to each Decision Module. But no matter how you distribute the time, you will find these modules a convenient way to schedule the work for a large project.

Decision Module A: Planning, Phase 1 *(Decisions 1 through 4)* These decisions make up the **writing situation**. Whatever you do, you need to make sure that you and your boss—or you and your work group—have the same notion of the **writing situation**. Otherwise, you may find yourself conceptualizing the project differently—working, in effect, on different projects. You can use these first four decisions as a way of discussing the project when it's assigned.

Decision Module B: Planning, Phase 2 *(Decisions 5 through 8)* These decisions allow you to structure the message. Use them to collaborate with your work group to set up the project, brainstorm the results, and develop an approach to structuring the product. The various outline stages offer you talking papers you can share with your manager, to find out whether the project is developing in a suitable direction.

Decision Module C: Drafting *(Decisions 9 through 11)* These drafting decisions are entirely individual. Even when you are collaborating with a work group, you might well be working in this phase entirely alone. All to the good—if you have collaborated on the first two modules (Decisions 1 through 8), then you are ready to draft according to previous agreements. Decision 11 focuses on identifying and planning possible graphics for your report.

Decision Module D: Revising *(Decisions 12 through 14)* These decisions will help you ensure that the theme and purpose of your report are clear and apparent to a reader. The section on Quick Fixes will help you address finer points of style.

Other Applications of the Decision Cycle These final chapters will help you use the Decision Cycle in your work life.

When you plan a project, set up milestones for each of the

Decision Modules. As you work through the book, you will develop a sense of the time you need to complete a module. On your next project, check your delivery deadline and then work backwards from it to set milestone deadlines for each Decision Module. Software, like the **Harvard Project Manager**, can help you organize your writing project and see how one slipped deadline will affect your entire schedule.

Make sure that you allow for the learning curve in the planning modules. Particularly if you are collaborating with others, you will need time to let the process work. And if you are pressed for time, remember that the planning modules are the ones you can least afford to stint. Making the early decisions systematically helps to ensure that, when you get to revising, you won't have to start over again.

CHAPTER TWO

Planning

Getting Started

How do you get a writing project off the ground? People often talk about a writing project as if it were, say, a plane getting ready to take off. But think about what can happen to a plane if the pilot neglects to conduct a preflight check of the systems. If you were a passenger, you'd probably prefer that the pilot set the flaps properly, check the fuel, and get the weather report.

In the same way that getting a plane up into the air requires a series of decisions (some routine, some not), writing requires a series of decisions. To get your project off the ground, you will need answers to the following questions, all pertinent to the Decision Cycle:

1. Why am I writing this document?
2. Who will use this document?
3. What do I/don't I need to tell the reader?
4. What role do I need to play?
5. What are the relevant facts?
6. How do the relevant facts relate to each other?
7. What major statements do I want to make?
8. How can I predict the draft?

Getting It Together

These decisions constitute the **planning phase** of the writing process. Making them explicitly, one by one, can help you connect with other people in your organization whose input your project might need. For instance, you will always need information about the first four decisions from your manager, or you will need your manager to buy into the way you make these decisions. And when the project requires collaborating with colleagues, the work group needs to agree on all eight decisions before drafting.

Although the process of making these decisions will consume time up front in the project, making them will considerably reduce drafting and reviewing time. In fact, you will find that the total project time will not increase when you invest time in these planning decisions. On the contrary, these decisions will make your project take off—and the results will make you look good.

The following modules A and B offer the Planning Decisions one by one, with explanations of each, and worksheets to help you make each decision. Take the time to draft answers to each worksheet question. The process of answering in writing will actually help you overcome the blank page syndrome, because by the time you are ready to draft, you will have geared up for writing.

Module A: Planning, Phase 1

(Decisions 1 through 4)

This module focuses on the initial decisions you need to make about the writing situation.

Decision 1
Why Am I Writing This Document?

Your first decision about the writing situation is an important one. You must decide why you are writing. To do so, you need to distinguish your **communication purpose** from your **technical purpose**. Your technical purpose is to do whatever you have to do—such as conduct an analysis of a potential product's strengths and weaknesses in the marketplace—in order to know enough to write. Your communication purpose is to say whatever you need to say about what you know. In a marketing report, your communication purpose might be to make recommendations.

You can distinguish these two purposes in terms of what they require of you. For instance, your technical purpose might be

☐ to define,

☐ to solve,

☐ to test,

☐ to explore,

☐ to formulate.

Your communication purpose (based on whatever you have defined, solved, tested, explored, or formulated) might be

☐ to propose,

☐ to request,

☐ to recommend,

☐ to justify,

☐ to explain.

Think of it this way: your technical purpose involves *something* (whatever you did—such as a marketing analysis—to get information); your communication purpose involves *somebody* (whoever will read—and act on—what you write).

Scenario

Suppose you are an engineer assigned to discover the reason for high costs and failure rates in the prototype of your company's new widget-grommet. As you study the situation, you discover that the underlying cause is a fundamental design flaw. Employing some new technology, you figure out how to overcome the problem, but your solution will require production changes—and an initial outlay of more money. You know that your solution will save the company money in the long run.

Two Purposes

Your technical purpose in this assignment is to find out what's causing the high costs and failure rates. Your communication purpose is to persuade your company to spend the additional money to adopt your solution.

The Problem

Some writers find it difficult to make the shift from technical purpose to communication purpose. In reality, you may have spent considerable time and money getting the education or training required to fulfill your technical purposes. You may think of those purposes as your job, while the documentation that reports or explains or justifies these purposes is merely an afterthought to the so-called real work. But, in many cases, the work is only as good as the document that comes out of it. Why? Because the work doesn't exist for other people without the document.

The Solution

What can you do about this element of the writing process? In a technical project, consider your ultimate communication purpose from the start. In any project, you might depict the relationship between technical and communication purposes in the following manner:

**RELATIONSHIP BETWEEN
TECHNICAL AND COMMUNICATION PURPOSES**

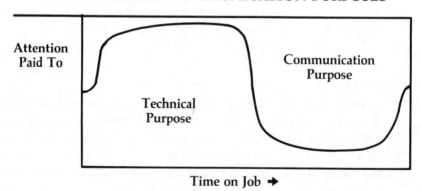

WRITING TO PLEASE YOUR BOSS

That is, as you start the job, you will be largely concerned with "What do I need to do?" As you move through the job, however, fulfilling your technical purpose, your focus should shift to your communication purpose, "What do I need to say?"

The Decision Worksheet
In this worksheet, you identify the problem that needs to be solved in your report and then distinguish between the technical purpose and the communication purpose.

Decision 1
Worksheet

Instructions: Write an answer to each question.

Statement of the Problem

Why do I need to do this job? What is at issue?

The company is incurring unacceptably high costs and failure rates on the phototype of the new widget-grommet.

Technical Purpose

What do I need to do in order to know what I need to know?

To solve problem — must study design; study production process; find out what is causing failure rates; must study production costs and determine what connection exists between failure rates and high costs. Must figure out how to reduce failure rates and costs.

Communication Purpose

What does my document need to do? What do I need to say in order for someone else to know?

Document must propose production changes and persuade my bosses to spend money for changes. (They're concerned about costs already!) Must justify outlay by explaining problem and demonstrating long-run costs to company — if my solution not accepted.

Decision 2
Who Will Use This Document?

Your second decision about the writing situation occurs because there are real people out there, a simple but often forgotten fact. They have their own reasons for reading, which may be largely different from your reasons for writing. Furthermore, their knowledge may not be the same as yours. Communication occurs when you bridge the gap between what's in your head and what's in your reader's head.

As you try to bridge that gap, you will find many obstacles. For one thing, your reader isn't present to let you know how well you're getting your points across; you have to make an educated guess. For another thing, you may have more than one reader to consider, and your readers may have different viewpoints. Again, you will have to make an educated guess about those viewpoints.

The worksheets for this decision will help you make those educated guesses, based on three assumptions you can make about your readers. One, none of your readers knows from the start exactly what you know. (Otherwise, why would you need to write anything?) Two, your readers may not know exactly why you're writing. And three, various readers may have different degrees of knowledge about your subject.

Scenario

Suppose you work for an environmental consulting firm and you need to do an asbestos removal report for the director of a charitable foundation. You did not perform the asbestos survey yourself; a team of two asbestos specialists surveyed the building. You are working from their survey notes, and consulting with them occasionally.

Your Primary Reader

The purpose of the report is to inform the director of the foundation about the problem he faces. Although he has some understanding of the dangers of asbestos, he is uninformed about the technical aspects of its removal. He probably has no idea of the dimensions of the problem, or what will be involved in solving it.

Among other things, he will have to understand the rationale behind whatever you propose, but he will be unacquainted with most of the technical terms involved in the procedure. The director, as the client, is your primary reader.

Specialist Readers

On the other hand, you are aware that the asbestos specialists—your working group—will review your report. To them, such a report is routine. You know that your report must satisfy the specialists with its accuracy. If you're not careful, you may catch yourself writing for these specialists—the readers with the least need for your document. But if you write primarily with them in mind, you run the risk of not communicating with your primary audience. You may confuse the foundation director in two ways: by assuming he understands your basic working assumptions (and therefore not explaining them), and by using technical terminology.

To solve such a problem, you can aim the report at the primary user, and include a technical appendix for the benefit of specialist readers. In this instance, it's a good idea. Although you don't know this fact in advance, the director will send the report to a member of the Board of Trustees, who happens to be an official of the U.S. Environmental Protection Agency.

Reviewers

Your firm's marketing manager will also review your report before it goes out. The marketing manager, while not an asbestos specialist, is quite familiar with the subject, having seen many such reports. But her review will consider the needs of your client, the foundation director. The marketing manager's job is to make sure your document is usable by the intended user, and, if the client isn't satisfied, she hasn't done her job. Because her job depends on the user's satisfaction, she will read with an element of self-protection in mind, and may be your most cautious and demanding reader. (Possibly, she has more experience than you in predicting unforeseen reactions by naive or politically sensitive readers.)

18

The Decision Worksheet

Worksheet A helps you identify the readers and what they know and don't know about your topic. Before you begin to draft, use it to make sure your document will be usable by its intended readers. Worksheet B helps you focus on your primary reader, the user of your document's information.

Decision 2
Worksheet A

Instructions: List all of your readers under Users and Reviewers. Then
fill in the chart for each reader.

	Need for Document	Knowledge of My Task	Level of Expertise	Mastery of Relevant Vocabulary
Users				
Director	high	very little	low	low
Member of Board	moderate	moderate	high	high
Reviewers				
Marketing Mgr.	low	moderate	moderate	moderate
My work group	low	high	high	high

Decision 2
Worksheet B

Instructions: Decide who is the most important reader for your document. Answer the following questions for that reader.

Key reader: _Director of foundation_

Role within the organization: _leader, prime decision maker, guiding light, controller of purse strings_

Why this reader needs my document: _must make informed decision that affects longrange safety of staff_

Reader's knowledge of my task: _has asked that survey be done and report submitted, but has little notion of procedures involved._

Reader's knowledge of technical area: _B.A. in English, worked in public relations has worked as teacher for 7 years; been Director for past 8 years._

Reader's education and professional experience: _only knowledge that an educated reader of daily news has. Little knowledge of technical terms._

Reader's attitudes that might bear on my document: _A little panicked at thought of cost and confusion involved in solving asbestos problem. Also concerned about justifying expenditure to Board of Trustees. Most concerned about health and safety._

Decision 3
What Do I/Don't I Need
to Tell the Reader?

Now that you have considered who is reading your document, you're ready to take a look at your subject matter through your reader's eyes. That is, you need to decide how to align your knowledge with your reader's needs. As an expert in your own subject matter—either because of extensive research, or because of your training and experience—you probably know a lot. Now you need to consider what you can safely assume your reader already knows.

Scenario

Suppose you're still working on the asbestos report, introduced in Decision 2. The asbestos specialists in your working group certainly understand the technical background of theory and method that allowed them to generate the information contained in the report. On the other hand, your client is relatively unsophisticated in the area.

Your Primary Reader's Needs

Your client is aware of having a technical problem, but would be unable to follow a technical explanation of your solution. He will need an explanation couched in terms he understands. (In fact, analogies might be particularly helpful to him.) You will have to explain any technical terms you use, and you might not be able to assume that the client will understand the reasons for what you recommend unless you explain your rationale. You will try to find where the common ground exists between the writer's knowledge (yours) and the reader's knowledge. Where that common ground ends, the reader's need for information begins. To help you supply the information the reader needs, you need to anticipate the questions your reader might have about the subject.

The Decision Worksheet

In this worksheet, you balance the assumptions you can make about the reader's knowledge against the information you need to offer the reader; that is, you weigh the knowledge the reader brings to the document against the questions the reader will have about the subject.

Decision 3
Worksheet

Instructions: List your readers in the left-hand column, and for each one list the assumptions you can make about what the reader knows. In the right-hand column, list the questions about the subject that each reader is likely to have.

Readers	Assumptions (what the reader already knows)	Questions (what you need to tell the reader)
1. Director	1. asbestos is dangerous	1. why? how? how much is here?
	2. there's a cost for removing it	2. how much? why?
	3. removal might disrupt operations	3. in what ways? for how long? how much disruption?
	4. good to remove asbestos	4. consequences if we don't?
2. Board Member	1. physical properties of asbestos	1. how much here?
	2. risks of not removing	2. legal risk? ethical risk?
	3. biological effects	3. extent of contamination here?
	4. dimensions of national problem	4. what effect on staff?
	5. aspects of asbestos management	5. costs, disruptions, public relations issues?

Decision 4
What Role Do I Need to Play?

You've already considered your purpose, who your readers are, and what they need and don't need to be told. Decision 4 focuses on the last consideration of the **writing situation**: how you will relate to your readers, how you, the writer, need to come across in your document. You must decide what role you will play in relation to the readers as you fulfill your purpose in writing.

Different Roles

Think about what you wear as you play different roles in your daily life. For instance, you very likely wear a jacket and tie, or a suit and heels, to work—but casual clothes, like a sweat suit, at home. Although comfortable and even functional, casual clothes seem inappropriate in most workplaces. They simply send the wrong signal about the role you are playing in the workplace. Similarly, you signal in your writing, usually through your tone, what role you are playing in relation to the reader, what stance you are taking in regard to your subject and purpose.

Scenario

Think back to the engineering report in Decision 1, in which your job is to persuade your company to invest money to fix something that's gone wrong. Your report will contain some unwelcome news for your own bosses. It requires them to spend more money in the short run to save money in the long run. In addition (just to complicate matters), your report will cause problems for the head of Design Engineering, who didn't catch the design flaw that caused the problem. In your report, you must come across as credible, helpful, a team player—with the best interests of the company at heart. You must also come across as objective. You don't want to be seen as merely out to get the Design Engineering staff.

The Decision Worksheet

The worksheet for Decision 4 helps you identify the roles you need to play in relation to your various readers. Use it each time you write to help you come across the way you want to.

Decision 4
Worksheet

Instructions: In the left-hand column, fill in your anticipated readers. Then describe what role you can appropriately play in relation to that reader.

Readers	Writer's Role in Relation to Reader
Your boss	trouble-shooter (problem-solver) team player (motivated by best interests of company)
Head of design engineering	expert (you know what you're talking about) colleague (not motivated by competition)

Module B:
Planning, Phase 2
(Decisions 5 through 8)

This module focuses on the decisions you need to make about collecting your data, grouping it into related units, and then structuring the information into an outline.

Decision 5
What Are the Relevant Facts?

Now that you've made Decisions 1 through 4, you've completed the preliminary thinking. You've made all the decisions you need to determine the **writing situation**, and you're ready to move further on around the Decision Cycle. You're ready to see what material you need to work with.

Identifying the Facts

Your document will not suddenly spring full-blown out of your head at this point. More likely, you will put it together out of ideas and information available to you: you will build it out of pieces. You are at the **facts** stage of the Decision Cycle, but before you can gather the facts, you need to return to the **writing situation** and consider what you know about the subject.

In functional writing, two things are true:

1. You almost always draw upon knowledge you have about your field to help you decide what facts you need to collect.

2. You almost always draw your information from multiple sources.

Scenario

You work for a market research company that specializes in real estate development. You have been asked to prepare an analysis of a resort site for possible vacation home development. The resort site is a "destination hotel," known as The Hawk's Nest, in Dalesville, North Carolina.

Drawing Upon Your Knowledge of the Field

Your knowledge of the topic comprises the given; usually it will consist of a theoretical framework or an understanding of what general areas need to be covered. In fact, you anticipated your reader's questions in Decision 3. Now you can use those questions to guide you in gathering information. Your background (either experience or education) tells you what new information you need to collect about your subject, in this case, The Hawk's Nest.

As a relatively new employee, you look at some old reports to remind yourself of the basic points that are covered by this type of report. You also rely on your previous experience, that is, the fact that you have already written three previous analyses for the company. You know the field: you've read past reports; you've written them yourself. Consequently, you know you need to deal with such areas as

- ☐ access
- ☐ facilities
- ☐ clientele.

Based on what you already know, you are even able to project three subcategories of facilities:

- ☐ sleeping
- ☐ eating
- ☐ playing.

These working categories allow you to limit the scope of your research. Now that you know what you're looking for about The Hawk's Nest, you're in a position to gather information.

Drawing Upon Multiple Sources

You cannot rely solely on the company library for information for this assignment. To get information in the areas that you've defined, you know that you need to

- ☐ request corporate and guest literature from The Hawk's Nest,
- ☐ request information from the state and county offices of economic development,

☐ look at maps,

☐ visit the site, and

☐ interview travel agents.

When these tasks are completed, you have the facts—but just the facts. Some of them are in the form of notes taken by a research assistant. Other information you've highlighted with a yellow marker in the literature you collected.

You and your assistant need to bring this material together so that you can analyze it.

Storyboarding

How do you bring your material together? You can use a method called storyboarding. Storyboarding is ideal for working with large bodies of data because it provides a flexible format in which to classify information for analysis. This method displays information in pieces small enough to be both seen and moved around easily. You may have used a version of storyboarding if you have worked with a group on a proposal.

To storyboard information, transfer your data from your different sources onto Post-it ™ brand notes (or similar gummed slips). Sort the Post-it ™ notes in groups according to the categories that you have identified. If you haven't identified categories, sort them according to similarity until categories emerge. As you group similar information, you may discover further categories you had not anticipated.

The worksheet of your first cut at grouping your data might look like the chart on pages 30 and 31.

Decision 5
Worksheet

Instructions: Go through your research notes or working papers and mark all the items of information you might conceivably use in your document. Write each item of information on an individual Post-it ™ note (the kind that sticks on paper, but can be removed and placed elsewhere). Don't censor yourself or edit the notes; your object at this stage is simply to generate a stockpile. When you have made a stockpile, assemble the Post-it ™ notes in storyboard fashion. You will find it helpful to spread them out on a large sheet of paper (flip-chart size). It can be rolled and stored for further work, it can be moved easily, and it can be hung on the wall.

Facilities			
eat	kitchen outdated	excellent dinner	only cold breakfast
	elegant dining room		
sleep	640 guest rooms	decayed elegance	small rooms
play	17.000 acres	18 hole golf course	stable horse trails
	27 miles hiking trails	3 heated pools	5 tennis courts no lights
	3 lakes stocked	wooded	no community center
Other	founded 1888	rebuilt 1914 after fire	can seat 3,800 people
can be snowbound	meeting rooms— 16	ballroom over 10,000 sq. ft.	entrance not well— marked
enter via residential streets	summer temp. 780 F	Dalesville: antique + craft center	hot springs + bath

Clientele	Access

40% guests are social guests	has own airport	I-40 across mountains
stay ~ 2 wks.	only private planes	
60% meeting guests	immediate access from US25	
stay ≈ 3-5 days	I-81 connects to US25 25 mi from Dalesville	
many have come since childhood	I-40 connects to US25 30 mi from Dalesville	
bring family	near Asheville	
23% guests from VA	Asheville has flights from DC, Richmond Atlanta	

8% various other states	15% guests from NC	Close to Research Triangle
7.5% NY	11% from MD	

Decision 6
How Do the Relevant Facts Relate to Each Other?

In this decision, you will determine the relevance of the facts to each other and to other groups of facts. You will be discovering new categories of information within the available material, and you will use storyboarding to construct your first outline.

Scenario

In Decision 5, you and your assistant made a storyboard to group your Hawk's Nest Post-it ™ notes under the three preliminary categories: **access**, **facilities**, and **clientele**. You discover that you have almost three times as many Post-it ™ notes in the facilities category as you have in either of the other two. First of all, some of your facilities information doesn't fit under your original "sleeping," "eating," "playing" subcategories. You just threw those notes into an "other" category, but now you need to deal with them. You try to reorganize them into categories, and now your storyboard looks like this:

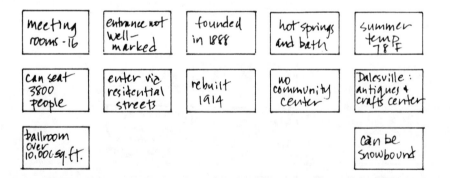

What Happens Next?

What happens next is almost impossible to lay out in a linear way. Why? Because the human brain is not linear; it works recursively. In other words, it touches on an idea, lets it go, makes connections unconsciously, comes back to an idea, finds a new one, and suddenly you see an order or a way to organize things that just wasn't there before.

How did you do it? There's no formula (although sometimes it does seem like magic), so there's no easy way to tell you what will work every time. Instead, you help your brain by priming the pump, by providing your brain with the opportunity to do what it does best: think. And you do this by breaking tasks into smaller, more discrete units.

When you work like this, you are breaking new information (about The Hawk's Nest, in this case) into units small enough to allow your brain to call up what you already know. What you call up might be another report you've read, something you learned in a class, or examples of good writing. The combination of the old and the new allows you to organize your new information.

Because of the way storyboarding works, it can greatly facilitate a group thinking process. Note that if you are working with colleagues at this stage, a storyboard allows each person access to all the information in a visual format. In addition, each person has an opportunity to contribute changes—with no penalty for a false start. If you move a Post-it ™ note to the wrong category, it's simple to move it back.

Back to The Hawk's Nest

Now go back to the storyboard. When you look at your other divisions, your assistant suggests separating "playing" into "recreation facilities" and "setting." You write them on large (3" × 5") Post-it ™ notes. You move the information about meeting rooms into the "sleeping" category and rename the category "The Grand Hotel," subdivided into "meetings" and "resort." You still have two groups left. One is a small group concerning the entrance, which you just know is important and deserves attention, even if there's not much to say about it. You decide to call it "approach." You think the other group may have something to do with "setting."

Getting the Big Chunks

So, what does your storyboard look like so far? You array your big Post-it ™ notes on a second sheet of flip-chart paper, like this.

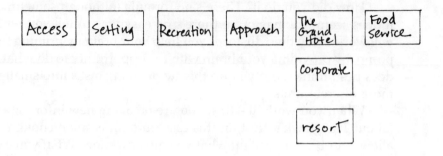

Then you realize that this new array (of your old "facilities" group) could be called "site evaluation." You write this phrase on a large Post-it ™ notes and place it at the top of your paper, like this:

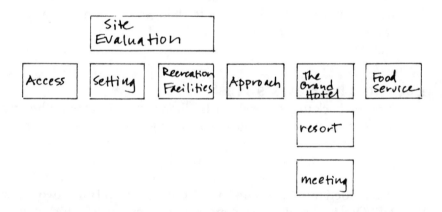

Getting Some Order

You want to put these categories into some kind of order, which could be one of importance, one of visibility, or one of time. You decide that you will put your categories into the logical order of how a guest would experience The Hawk's Nest. You rearrange your Post-it ™ note like this:

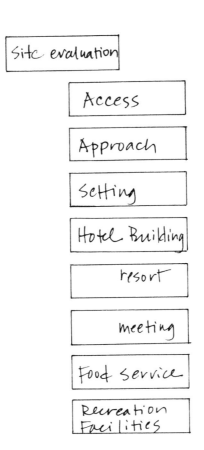

Making the Outline

Does the pattern look familiar? You're right. If you add Roman numerals and letters, you have an outline—a topic outline. You've worked from your storyboard to produce an outline. You might, in fact, copy your outline onto a sheet of paper to formalize it.

    I. Site Evaluation
        A. Access
        B. Approach
        C. Setting
        D. The Grand Hotel
            1. resort
            2. meeting

E. Food Service

F. Recreation Facilities

What's Next?

You go through this same storyboarding process for each of your groupings of facts. As you complete each section, you have an additional part of your topic outline.

For your report on The Hawk's Nest, your topic outline might look like this one:

TOPIC OUTLINE FOR THE HAWK'S NEST MOUNTAIN RESORT

    I. Site Evaluation

        A. Access

        B. Approach

        C. Setting

        D. The Grand Hotel

            1. resort

            2. meeting

        E. Food Service

        F. Recreation Facilities

   II. Visitor Profile

        A. Potential Buyers

        B. Social Guests

        C. Group Guests

  III. Evaluation

        A. Strengths

            1. Reputation

            2. Amenity Package

            3. Setting

        B. Weaknesses

            1. Narrow Target Market

            2. Distance from Major Markets

What Else Can You Do?

You can do one more activity that will help you prepare to write. Array your individual facts under each appropriate heading. Now you have combined facts with a first level of concepts. You're moving toward completion of the **message** portion of the Decision Cycle.

The example below shows only the first part—Site Evaluation—of the outline with its supporting detail.

TOPIC OUTLINE FOR THE HAWK'S NEST MOUNTAIN RESORT

    I. Site Evaluation

        A. Access

        B. Approach

        C. Setting

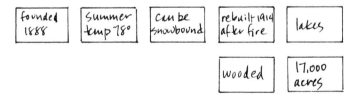

        D. The Grand Hotel

            1. resort

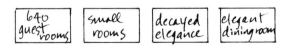

2. meeting

| 16 meeting rooms | 10,000 sq ft ballroom | can seat 3,800 |

E. Food Service

| kitchen outdated | excellent dinner | only cold breakfast |

F. Recreation Facilities

| hot springs + bath | Dalesville: antiques + craft center | 3 stocked lakes | no community center |

Decision 6
Worksheet

Instructions: Work with your storyboard. Examine your first group-ings of Post-it ™ notes to see whether your preliminary categories are viable. Look for exceptionally large bodies of data under one category—a sign that the category needs to be divided. Also look for relevance of facts to each other within a category. If some seem not to belong together, put them in a different category. Regroup until two things seem possible:

1. all facts within a category can be arranged in a meaningful order, and
2. all categories can be arranged in a meaningful order.

Decision 7
What Major Statements
Do I Want to Make?

Now that you have determined the topics and the basic facts for each topic, this decision requires that you focus them. Using your storyboard, you will be moving from topic areas to statements as you complete the **concepts** portion of the Decision Cycle and move toward **structure**. You will be synthesizing the information under each of your topic headings into a single nutshell statement—an overview. You should end up with the major statements for your document in order—a statement outline.

A statement outline differs significantly from a topic outline. While a topic outline is a tool you can use to organize your own thinking, a statement outline is a tool you can use to organize your approach to the reader. You might say a topic outline is for the writer, and a statement outline is for the reader.

When you have put together a statement outline, you will have written a "talking paper" for your report—something that gives you a rough idea of what you want to say and where you want to say it. If necessary, you could draft from this outline or dictate a rough draft into a dictaphone.

Scenario

As in Decision 6, there's no formula to tell you how to determine your major statements. But bear in mind that these statements should provide answers to the reader questions you identified in Decision 3. Again, you bring your past knowledge, your current expertise, a whole array of experiences—including working through Decision 6—to bear on each portion of the outline.

Look at your storyboard/outline. You know these facts belong together; now you're trying to articulate why. You're trying to answer the question, "What's the point of these details?"

Look at the facts grouped under the heading "Access" in your topic outline.

What do you want to say *about* all of these facts? How do these facts combine to make a point that you will be able to use in your report on The Hawk's Nest? The facts seem to be about driving or flying to The Hawk's Nest, but what do these facts say? Aha! The light bulb goes on:

☐ Highways and planes offer easy access to The Hawk's Nest.

Even if this isn't a perfect way of capturing of what you mean, it's a start. Repeat this process for each section. Skip around if it helps. Do the easy ones first, then the more difficult ones. You may even regroup some of the facts or rename some of the headings on your storyboard. As you do this, you're moving through **concepts** to complete the **message** portion of the Decision Cycle.

When you have completed a statement for each topic, you are ready to move across the line into the **structure** portion of the Decision Cycle. How do you do this? Simply arrange your Post-it ™ note statements in hierarchical order.

Once you have arranged the statements, you have a statement outline. A statement outline for the project might look like the following example.

STATEMENT OUTLINE FOR THE HAWK'S NEST MOUNTAIN RESORT

I. Site Evaluation

    A. Accessibility is the primary advantage of The Hawk's Nest.

    B. The approach to the resort needs to be enhanced.

    C. The Grand Hotel can serve as a focal point for vacation home development.

    D. Recreation facilities can form the nucleus of a community activity center.

    E. The grounds are a unique asset in the vacation home market.

II. Visitor Profile

    A. Guests at the resort form the logical pool of buyers.

    B. Social guests are a strong potential market.

    C. Group guests are a secondary potential market.

III. Evaluation

    A. The Hawk's Nest offers four competitive strengths.

        1. Its established reputation for quality is its chief strength.

        2. The amenity package is attractive to potential buyers.

        3. The natural beauty of the setting is a significant asset for development.

        4. Strong customer base constitutes a prequalified market.

    B. The Hawk's Nest faces two constraints for resort-oriented residential development.

        1. Qualified buyers represent a narrow target market.

        2. Distance from major cities detracts from marketability.

Decision 7
Worksheet

Instructions: Use 3" × 5" Post-it ™ notes for this stage of your storyboard. Write each of your topic headings on a 3" × 5" Post-it ™ note. Look at each topic and see what answers it suggests to your reader's questions about the subject. (See Decision 3.) Expand the topic into a complete statement that answers the questions, then arrange the statements in order. Use the order of your topic outline first. To see if the statements make sense in that order, read them aloud. They should tell the "story" you are trying to convey. If they don't make sense in that order, try changing the order or the statements themselves.

In moving from topics to statements, you should be able to accomplish two things:

1. say what you mean *about* each of your topics, and
2. arrange the points in order. (You may find at this stage that the order of your categories needs to change.)

Decision 8
How Can I Predict the Draft?

Can you draft from a statement outline like the one in Decision 7? Sure—if you are working on your own. In that case, a statement outline is all the preparation you may need before drafting. But if, as is so often the case in an organization, you are collaborating with others, you will need another step. You will need an **expanded outline**. An expanded outline makes the connections among pieces of information explicit and sets the tone for the piece. It predicts the draft with greater assurance than does a statement outline.

An expanded outline is a variation of a statement outline. It includes the **executive summary** (or whatever preliminary piece is intended to provide an overview); all titles, captions, and subcaptions; introductory paragraphs for each chapter or major division; and topic sentences for major paragraphs. Because the introductory paragraphs are fully written out, an expanded outline also establishes the tone of the written product. This advantage helps several writers divide up the chapters and still approximate the same tone.

Scenario

You work with the research assistant to develop an expanded outline. And it's a good thing you do. Before you can draft chapter III, you are called out of town on another assignment. Your research assistant is able to draft Chapter III from the outline.

Here is an expanded outline (minus the executive summary) that could be generated from your analysis of The Hawk's Nest.

EXPANDED OUTLINE FOR THE HAWK'S NEST MOUNTAIN RESORT

The success of possible new development will principally depend on how well The Hawk's Nest can compete with other locations for resort-oriented vacation home projects. Accordingly, this discussion will analyze the advantages of the site and the nature of the potential buyer pool. It will conclude with an evaluation of the competitive position of The Hawk's Nest in the market.

    I.   Site Evaluation
        The Hawk's Nest Mountain Resort consists of a turn-of-

the-century destination hotel, built in the grand manner, set on a 17,000-acre property. Located in charming Dalesville, North Carolina, near a major national park, it offers hot springs, streams, waterfalls, and hiking trails, along with striking mountain scenery.

    A. Access is the primary advantage of The Hawk's Nest.

    B. The approach to the resort needs to be enhanced.

    C. The Grand Hotel can serve as a focal point for vacation home development.

    D. Recreation facilities can form the nucleus of a community activity center.

    E. The grounds are a unique asset in the vacation home market.

II. Visitor Profile

Guests at the resort form the logical pool of buyers. These guests are either social guests or group guests. Of these two, social guests constitute a more significant market for vacation home development.

    A. Social guests are a strong potential market.

    B. Group guests are a secondary potential market.

III. Evaluation

The Hawk's Nest enjoys several advantages, including its reputation for quality, attractive amenities, striking mountain setting, and strong customer base. These may serve to offset the disadvantages of a narrow target market and distance from major cities.

    A. The Hawk's Nest offers four competitive strengths.

        1. Its established reputation for quality is its chief strength.

        2. The amenity package is attractive to potential buyers.

        3. The natural beauty of the setting is a significant asset for development.

        4. Strong customer base constitutes a prequalified market.

    B. The Hawk's Nest faces two constraints for resort-oriented residential development.

1. Qualified buyers represent a narrow target market.
2. Distance from major cities detracts from marketability.

When Should You Use an Expanded Outline?

An expanded outline is useful under three sets of circumstances:

☐ when the information is extremely complex or delicate;

☐ when the project needs predrafting review; or

☐ when the document is lengthy and will be divided up among several writers who need to coordinate their efforts.

Is It Worth It?

Does this kind of outline take a lot of time and effort to produce? Yes. Is it worth it? You bet. Once you have produced an expanded outline, you have made all of the major writing decisions. What's left are specific examples, word choices, and sentence structures, the most individual and particular decisions.

Your drafting time will be decreased considerably, and—perhaps even more significantly—your review and rewrite time will be decreased. You will have been able to get your manager or colleagues to buy into a realistic prediction of the draft, or you will have been able to coordinate realistically with your colleagues. No major surprises should show up in the written product, which should require only fine tuning.

Here's an example of the first draft you might get if you wrote from the expanded outline. Consider how little actual time this draft might take, once the expanded outline is in place.

Draft Report on the Hawk's Nest Mountain Resort

The success of possible new development will principally depend on how well The Hawk's Nest can compete with other locations for resort-oriented vacation home projects. Accordingly, this discussion will analyze the advantages of the site and the nature of the potential buyer pool. It will conclude with an evaluation of the competitive position of The Hawk's Nest in the market.

Site Evaluation. The Hawk's Nest Resort consists of a turn-of-the-century destination hotel, built in the grand manner, set on a 17,000-acre property. Located in charming Dalesville, North Carolina, near a major national park, it offers hot springs, streams, waterfalls, and hiking trails, along with striking mountain scenery.

Access is the primary advantage of The Hawk's Nest. Dalesville and The Hawk's Nest are easily accessible by automobile. Interstate 40 (I-40) connects with U.S. 25 an easy thirty miles from Dalesville, providing access to the North Carolina Piedmont region. Interstate 81 (I-81) connects with U.S. Route 25 only twenty-five miles from Dalesville, providing access to the entire eastern seaboard.

These two interstates reach a number of suitable potential markets. I-40 is a major east-west corridor, which offers direct accessibility from Asheville and slightly more distant accessibility from the Research Triangle of Chapel Hill, Durham, and Raleigh. I-81, also an important corridor, runs north-south and provides direct access from more distant areas such as Virginia, Pennsylvania, and upstate New York, along with south-central states such as Tennessee and Georgia. The Hawk's Nest is thus easily accessible both to the eastern seaboard and south central states.

The Hawk's Nest is also accessible by air. Although of limited size, the resort's private airfield, Jefferson Field, accommodates private planes. In addition, nearby Asheville has commercial flights from a variety of major cities in the east.

Clearly, this air access is an advantage toward broadening the geographic reach of The Hawk's Nest to cities that are outside reasonable driving distance.

The approach to the resort needs to be enhanced. The entrance, via residential streets, is not well marked. In addition, the road leading into The Hawk's Nest should be repaved in order to make it more inviting to prospective buyers, and to improve the limited access during heavy snowfalls.

The scenic beauty of Piedmont North Carolina offers a multitude of options for vacationers. Located near a major national park, the resort offers hot springs and baths, streams, waterfalls, and hiking trails, along with striking mountain scenery. In addition, the town of Dalesville, average summer temperature 78 degrees Fahrenheit, features a nationally-renowned antique and crafts center.

The grounds are a unique asset in the vacation home market. Serving both the leisure and sports-minded, the resort offers the following amenities:

- [ ] an eighteen-hole golf course
- [ ] horse stables and trails
- [ ] three heated pools
- [ ] twenty-seven miles of hiking trails
- [ ] five tennis courts
- [ ] three stocked lakes.

It is recommended that a community activity center be built on the grounds as a means both to coordinate the recreation facilities and to provide a mid-day resting place for guests.

The Hawk's Nest's Grand Hotel can serve as the focal point for vacation home development. The hotel's 640 guest rooms are elegant, but small and in need of renovation. Sixteen meeting rooms, spacious and well-equipped, are also available.

The hotel's kitchen, though outdated, is expansive and well-built, with the capacity to hold several employees. An elegant dining room, decorated in a charming Victorian style, seats two hundred people. In addition to the large and elegant serving capacities of the resort's kitchen and dining room, the hotel also features an over 10,000 square foot ballroom. With these amenities, the Grand Hotel provides excellent marketing possibilities as a location for large parties and weddings.

Visitor Profile. The Hawk's Nest's strong customer base of social and group guests forms the logical pool of buyers. Of these two types of guests, social guests constitute a more significant market for vacation home development.

Social guests are a strong potential market. Currently, forty percent of the resort's clientele is comprised of social guests, who have an average stay of two weeks. Many of these guests bring their families, and many have been coming to The Hawk's Nest since childhood. This established, loyal core of guests provides an immediate group of likely prospective buyers.

Group guests are a secondary potential market. Making up sixty percent of the resort's clientèle, the average stay of the meeting guests is three to five days. These guests could be lured by both the resort's leisure and business amenities.

The clientele is composed primarily of guests from the eastern seaboard states:

- ☐ 23% from Virginia
- ☐ 15% from North Carolina
- ☐ 11% from Maryland
- ☐ 7.5% from New York
- ☐ 4.5% from New Jersey
- ☐ 2% from Pennsylvania
- ☐ 38% from other states.

The Hawk's Nest provides both ready accessibility and a remote vacation atmosphere to its established East Coast client base. Thus, a campaign aimed at this lucrative pool of prospective buyers offers many marketing possibilities.

Evaluation. The Hawk's Nest enjoys several advantages, including its reputation for quality, attractive amenities, striking mountain setting, and strong customer base. These may serve to offset the disadvantages of a narrow target market and distance from major cities.

The Hawk's Nest offers four competitive strengths. Its established reputation for quality is its chief strength, and has kept generations of guests returning since it was built in 1888. The amenity package is attractive to potential buyers. The resort offers excellent facilities for both leisure and business purposes, and the capacity to provide these services to large and small groups. Finally, the natural beauty of the setting is a significant asset for development. With its striking scenery, both on its grounds and in its outlying areas, and with its varied amenities utilizing the land, The Hawk's Nest provides strong development potential.

Decision 8
Worksheet

Instructions: Add the following elements to your statement outline: an executive summary (or abstract or digest) and an introductory paragraph for each section. You already have captions and topic sentences from the statement outline in Decision 7.

A PLANNER'S BILL OF RIGHTS

1. You have the right to full information about the writing situation.
2. You have the right to program sufficient planning time into the project.
3. You have the right to plan when you are under deadline pressure.
4. You have the right to say "Yes, I'm writing" when you're planning.
5. You have the right to Post-it ™ notes.
6. You have the right to negotiate decisions with other members of the work group.
7. You have the right to your manager's feedback on the planning decisions.
8. You have the right to reconsider your planning documents.
9. You have the right to complete your planning process.
10. You have the right to feel some anxiety about getting finished as you plan.

CHAPTER THREE

Collaborating With Your Boss

You and your manager probably have a common objective: to get the written product out the door, and, so to speak, off to work. Unfortunately, you and your manager may have different ideas of how to get to the door—or even which door you're aiming for. In a situation such as this, your draft can get lost in what seems like a maze of review changes, never finding the way out.

You want your draft to count. You want to avoid doing useless work, and you want to avoid starting over. In fact, you need to ensure that when you sit down to draft, you are moving in the right direction. What good is all the planning you've done if you have to redo it after you've gone to the trouble of drafting?

To make it worthwhile, you need to confirm your planning with your boss at this point. Managers are often attuned to the organizational issues represented by the writing situation on the Decision Cycle. For this reason, you need to share your thinking before you draft, so that you can get feedback on your planning strategy. You might accomplish this sharing in formal or informal ways, depending on the nature of your planning, the nature of your boss, and the nature of your organization.

What Kind of Planning to Share

You can get two kinds of feedback: formal and informal. And, while you need feedback on all of your planning decisions, some of your planning documents are more suited to exposure than others.

Formal Feedback. You do need explicit feedback on at least two specific planning documents: your statement of purpose (Decision 1) and your statement outline (Decision 7).

Getting feedback on your statement of purpose allows you to determine something very important: that your boss and you have the same expectations of the project. If you neglect to determine this point, your draft may bring you more trouble than relief once it's finished. In fact, starting off in the wrong direction can cause you grief in two ways. In the first place, once you've drafted, you're invested in your way of thinking. As one of our clients said, "Once it's in writing, it's hard to throw it away." Even if you understand the new direction your boss wants, it's simply harder to go that way, because you've set your thinking. In the second place, your reputation as a productive writer may be jeopardized by a draft that misses the mark. Unfair or not, your boss may judge your productivity on how close you come to his own thinking and how fast you get there.

Getting feedback on your statement outline allows you to determine something else: that your logic meets your boss's expectations. If you have missed something important, or failed to emphasize something crucial, or given too much emphasis to something inconsequential, a statement outline allows your boss to catch the potential problem. It allows your boss to see not only what direction you're moving in, but also what ground you're covering.

Of course, the expanded outline, if you've done one, is the ideal planning document to share with your boss. It allows your boss to see not only what direction you're moving in and what ground you're covering, but also what stance you're taking, what tone you'll be using in your draft. It's the closest thing you can offer to a draft without actually making the investment of drafting.

And speaking of outlines, what about sharing your topic outline? On this point, be careful: topic outlines have pitfalls. Statement and expanded outlines are oriented to the reader, in that they predict the structure of your presentation. Topic outlines, on the other hand, are oriented to the writer, in that they help organize material and clarify the writer's early thinking. As such, topic outlines may not reflect the structure of the presentation—you're not that far yet. If you get your manager to sign off on a topic outline, you may each go away from the meeting with very different ideas of what the product will look like.

Informal Feedback. Some other planning decisions may be harder to share. For instance, while every good writer performs audience analysis (consciously and unconsciously), you might have reasons not to go public with a document that characterizes your readers. Precisely because such a planning document can reflect—and help you respond to—political sensitivities, you need to be sensitive to the possibility that it could be misinterpreted. You still need feedback from your manager about the accuracy of your perceptions about your audience, but use discretion in sharing your decision worksheets. In some circumstances, the feedback you need is best obtained informally, in an oral exchange. An "Oh, by the way. . ." at the water cooler might kick off such a meeting.

Dealing with Managerial Styles

Do these warnings seem to imply something negative about managers—that they're waiting to thwart you at every turn? It's easy to fall into that kind of thinking in an organization, especially in a very hierarchical one with an extended review process. And if your communication with your manager is not especially good, the problems can certainly multiply in the writing process.

The truth about managers is that they struggle with writing too. While your manager may have reached his or her current position partly due to writing skills, skill in writing does not guarantee skill in talking about writing. And, while many managers receive training in management skills, they are largely on their own in dealing with the problems of the writing process. In fact, your efforts to communicate your planning decisions may actually help your boss manage you better.

What if your boss throws up barriers to communicating about your writing project, barriers that he or she is not even aware of? The following descriptions of writing management styles may ring a few bells about your own manager, and you may be able to overcome the barriers by following the suggestions listed below.

☐ **"I'll know what I want when I see it."**

This manager *may* in fact be a very good writer—but an unconscious writer. This manager very likely depends heavily on drafting to make writing decisions, and consequently is not a conscious planner. This manager is asking you to clarify his or her own thinking about the project, and is likely to treat a draft as the beginning of the writing process, when to you it feels closer to the end. To this manager, the draft is a fluid and he or she is inclined to pour the draft back and forth until it looks right. Unfortunately, to you the draft is already a solid.

This attitude causes problems of which the manager is not aware. This manager may enthusiastically fix on something in your draft that suggests a new direction for the project to him or her. In some cases, the attitude leads to your starting over after doing a good deal of work.

Suggestion. You can avoid this situation by sharing your planning decisions early on. Since this manager is looking for clarification, he or she may be more receptive than some other managers to anything perceived as helping move the thought process.

☐ **"If I want it to turn out right, I'll have to do it myself."**

This manager is the familiar figure of management development case studies—the one who hasn't learned to delegate and may have control issues to work out. But as a writer, this manager may lack confidence, even though on the surface this attitude seems arrogant. This manager possibly doubts his or her own understanding of the project, and consequently the ability to articulate his or her requirements. And possibly this manager has experience in the past with inadequate staff, and has good reason for pessimism. This pessimism will manifest itself as doubt about your own capacities to perform. You need to be aware of this manager's predisposition to see your work as inadequate.

Suggestion. Defend against this style by getting as much information about early decisions as possible from this manager—especially the purpose statement. If he or she is confirmed in pessimism, your manager might gloss over this area, then regard a draft that misses the mark as no more than he or she expected. In fact, share whatever early planning documents you can get your manager to look at, to help build a positive attitude toward the progress of the project.

☐ **"It should be right the first time—it shouldn't need any changes."**
Boy, do you want your first draft to be on target for this manager! His or her attitude implies an intolerance for process, the notion that changes equal mistakes. A more sophisticated writer understands that written products evolve, but you're not likely to change this manager's mind overnight.

Suggestion. You want to be rigorous in following the Decision Method to perform for this manager. Be sure to get sign-off on a statement or expanded outline before you attempt to draft.

☐ **"If I could figure it out when I was new, they can figure it out too."**
This attitude sees work as a series of initiation rituals, and may belong to a relatively inexperienced manager—one who is still trying to figure out his or her own job. This manager may actually be saying, "If I knew how to give more information about the project up front, I would do it." The Decision Method can give this manager a vehicle for sharing what he or she knows.

Suggestion. You may be surprised—and pleased—at the results you get if you attempt to brainstorm the early decisions together. What you want to do is share your decision-making process. As with the "I'll know what I want when I see it" manager, you are helping this manager clarify his or her thinking. In this case, rather than helping to clarify thinking about the project, you are helping to clarify the manager's role.

☐ **"A Ph.D. [or a CPA, or a senior programmer, or a law associate] should know what to do without asking too many questions about the project."**
This attitude is similar to the previous manager's—but more entrenched. (It's where the previous manager is headed if someone doesn't help.) You can simply handle this attitude with tact.

Suggestion. You still need feedback about your planning decisions, but offer them as formally as possible. Don't present them as questions; rather present them as formal, interim documents representing your current thinking about the project. To this manager, questions betray ignorance—but your planning documents will represent tangible results and measurable progress toward the goal. You may actually find that this manager is impressed by your meticulous attention to planning.

Two Sides of the Same Coin

Communication difficulties between you and your manager may represent two sides of the same coin. When researchers interviewed managers and staff at one organization about writing, they found that managers and staff were remarkably consistent in the topic of their complaints. (See figure .) The actual complaints, however, are mirror-images of each other.

Communication throughout the project might resolve this dilemma. What do you need to communicate about? Both you and your manager need to be working from the same objective standards for the quality of a draft; you need to have the same perspective about the writing situation and about what needs to be said and not said; and you need to understand each other's working constraints. In other words, you both have to recognize that you're working toward the same goal.

The Conflict between Manager and Staff

Manager/Reviewer	Staff/Writer
1. I have to fix a lot of bad prose.	1. He tries to put it in his style.
2. He throws rough drafts at me.	2. He won't tell me what he wants.
3. It takes three or four recycles.	3. I don't understand his criticisms.
4. He doesn't spend any time writing.	4. I spend too much time writing.
5. It takes forever to edit this stuff.	5. It sits on his desk forever.
6. He's reluctant to write up results.	6. I can't get to writing because he's always giving me something else to do.
7. This needs to advance company objectives.	7. I want to show what I've been doing.
8. This better be good because my boss is looking at it.	8. I don't know who/what this is for.
9. I don't know how good this needs to be.	9. I don't know how good this needs to be.

Paradis, James, et al, "Writing at Exxon ITD: Notes on the Writing Environment of an R & D Organization," in Writing in Nonacademic Settings (New York: W. W. Norton and Company, Inc., 1985) p. 301.

CHAPTER FOUR

Drafting

How to Eat an Elephant

Drafting represents the stage many writers dread the most. If you're used to thinking of the drafting stage as **WRITING**, you may picture this stage as swallowing the project whole, like a boa constrictor digesting an elephant. The need to make fundamental decisions about a project holds up some writers at this point.

But unless you're a boa constrictor, the best way to eat an elephant is one bite at a time. You've begun that process by making the previous eight decisions and sharing at least Decisions 1 and 7 with your manager. In fact, the next step will be easier now than you ever thought it could be. You've made the central decisions that will allow you to draft your document. In writing words down and organizing them into a structure, you've accomplished a great deal. Most notably, you no longer have a blank page to face.

You may dread the drafting phase if you overestimate what you need to accomplish, especially if your comfort pattern puts most of your resources into drafting. For instance, when you try to get *only* the right words down on paper, you may encounter a writing block. For many projects, you will do best if you use drafting to achieve a rough cut, something you can reshape to your purposes in the revising process. (Remember, one bite at a time.)

Of course, in keeping with the recursive nature of the writing process, drafting includes some elements of revising. But for maximum efficiency, try to minimize the extent to which you revise as you draft. In other words, don't try to make all the remaining decisions now. Subtle decisions about word choice and sentence structure can be left to the revising phase. At this stage, you just want to get something down on paper that you can work with. Remember, you've done a lot of work already to prepare for this rough cut.

On the other hand, though, you don't want to underestimate this stage either. Now that you're about to draft, you'll be juggling a lot of balls in the air, and this juggling requires equilibrium and concentration. You need to prepare yourself psychologically for this procedure, and the next two decisions will help you do that.

Module C:
Drafting
(Decisions 9 and 10)

This module focuses on two aspects of drafting a document: managing your environment and your time.

Decision 9
How Can I Manage My Environment?

Some organizations seem to foster a sort of writing machismo: a myth that, if you're really good, you should be able to write poised on a high stool with a yellow pad and pencil while a jackhammer is going next door. Obviously, these are not circumstances that foster concentration, much less equilibrium. Instead, this myth often fosters writer's block. Managing your writing environment is one way to ensure that when you sit down to write, you'll get up with a draft.

Place

Your first task in managing your environment is to find a place where you can achieve relative quiet and minimize interruptions. While absolute quiet and privacy are rarely obtainable, you might consider at least having your telephone calls held. If you can, close the door. If you can't, you might try a change of scene. Is there a library you can use? Or even the company cafeteria at off hours can give you an opportunity to escape routine pressures long enough to get started. Come in early, stay late, or work at home when you have a draft to produce. Remember, none of these alternatives will necessarily involve days at a time. Since you've made your major decisions, you'll minimize the drafting time.

Tools

Second, make sure you have the tools you need. If possible, try to use a word processor. Even if you start by using it as a sophisticated typewriter, you will soon find the flexibility it gives you indispensable. If you are not working at a word processor, indulge your preference for unlined paper or a fountain pen. Have file folders and paper clips available to organize the volume of paper you have now enabled yourself to produce.

Comfort

Third, make yourself as comfortable as possible. Make sure you have enough light. Make sure you have space to spread out—drafting generates paper. If having coffee or cookies available helps keep you focused on the draft, have them. (Remember, once again, you've minimized the drafting time. This won't take forever.)

Movement

Fourth, move around once in a while. Although you should sit for at least twenty minutes at a time, research shows that getting up once in a while actually helps promote creativity. How often have you gotten up to get a cup of coffee, and arrived at a brilliant idea, or the solution to a problem, halfway across the room? Chances are you thought of it because of—not in spite of—getting up.

Attitude

If you've managed your external environment well, it may be easier to manage your internal environment. Primarily, you want to remember the goal of drafting: to get a first cut. It doesn't have to be perfect; it just has to be done. That's all you want. Once you have words down on a page, you'll be able to go back and revise and refine your thoughts, but for now—write.

Decision 10
How Can I Manage My Time?

If you've used the Decision Method, drafting won't take forever—but don't underestimate the time it will take. Drafting is still going to take work, and you want to be prepared for it. Allow yourself some psychological warm-up time by reviewing your planning documents to remind yourself of the writing situation and the structure of your message. Then follow the suggestions below.

Choose Your Best Time

Although you have simplified the task by explicit planning, drafting is still a complex activity. You will need to be as psychologically sharp as you can be. For this reason, you need to reserve your best times of day for drafting. You probably know whether you're a morning person or a night person, and this perception gives you a place to start. If you work best early in the morning or late at night, reserve those periods for drafting. Even if you must do your work during the confines of a nine-to-five day, you still will have some times that are best times. Try to draft during those hours.

Work for Ninety Minutes at a Time

Researchers maintain that the human body works in metabolic cycles of ninety minutes. In some cycles you feel up, in some you feel down. (Morning people, for instance, tend to crash in mid-afternoon.) Try to time your drafting not only to take in your best cycles, but to make maximum use of them. This means two things: first, stick to the task of drafting for ninety minutes at a time, and, second, take a break every ninety minutes—a real break that allows your brain to recharge. At your best times of day, you can probably successfully draft for two ninety-minute cycles back to back, but don't expect good results if you try to do this during your down time. Forcing yourself will probably result in wads of paper in your wastebasket.

A DRAFTER'S BILL OF RIGHTS

1. You have the right to schedule time to draft (just as you would schedule a meeting).
2. You have the right to privacy.
3. You have the right to quiet.
4. You have the right to proper tools.
5. You have the right to enough space and light.
6. You have the right to screen calls, even with an answering machine.
7. You have the right to take a break every ninety minutes.
8. You have the right to move around if you need to.
9. You have the right to PLAN before you draft.
10. You have the right to change the plan as you draft.

Just Write

Don't worry too much at this stage about how your draft sounds. You can sort out word choices and sentence structures later, after you produce a rough cut. Come back to these issues in the revising stage.

Decision 11
What Parts of the Story Can I Tell Visually?

For many people, visual aids are just that—aids, supplements, decorations, a kind of "added value" for a report. In truth, visual aids are **added** value, but they need to be integrated into the text, not merely applied. The visual image in American society is very powerful. Advertising campaigns are built around visual images that are intended to convey far more than information about a product. Think about the latest round of perfume and blue jeans ads; rest assured that the advertisers are trying to sell their products through more than an appeal to their consumers' minds only. Companies like Exxon and IBM invested a great deal of money before changing their logos because these companies realize the importance of their visual image. Consider that when *Lawrence of Arabia* played recently in Washington, D.C., theater owners reported that concession sales of soft drinks increased significantly, an increase which they attributed to "all that sand."

Visual Aids Help Sell Your Points

You may not be trying to sell jeans, perfume, or soft drinks, but in corporate communication visual aids are equally powerful. They can help you present your report more persuasively and more efficiently to your reader. Visual aids can help you more clearly describe objects, simplify and clarify concepts, show trends and relationships quickly and efficiently to a reader, and, in many cases, as you've heard before, they can be "worth a thousand words."

But good use of graphics requires that you think about incorporating graphics early in the project. You need to think *visually* as well as *verbally*. You want to be thinking about when and where to incorporate and integrate visual aids into your project as you deal with the facts of the report. To begin, you will need to consider for each visual aid three of the elements of the writing situation: What's my subject? Who's my reader? What's my purpose?

What's My Subject?

Your choice of visual aids is determined by the subject matter, but getting to the subject matter can be tricky. As you go through your details from Decisions 5 and 6, you can think about ideas for visual aids by following these five LOOK FORS:

1. LOOK FOR physical objects that could help to explain a point. You might consider objects that your reader could be unfamiliar with or, perhaps, an object that you are suggesting a change for, like your company's widget-grommet.

2. LOOK FOR concepts or ideas that you could show, like an organizational chart or work plan and schedule or the steps in the organization's review process. These visual aids can help a reader get a feel for intricacy or time.

3. LOOK FOR relationships among data that you might be able to chart to emphasize a point, like a trend in sales or enrollments. A good visual aid could help your reader see your point immediately.

4. LOOK FOR evidence that you might present visually to

WRITING TO PLEASE YOUR BOSS

make a persuasive point. Remember that visual aids are emphasizers; they draw attention to anything they portray. For instance, remember The Hawk's Nest report included a point about the unobtrusiveness of the entrance. A photograph of the obscured entrance could certainly underscore your point.

5. LOOK FOR detailed information that could be organized into a visual aid for simpler use and reference. You might summarize a series of points that your report has made and that you want readers to remember.

Once you've identified some potential data that you might use in a visual aid, then you're ready to move onto the next question.

Who Is My Reader?

Just as information about your various readers affected what you needed to say and didn't need to say about your subject in Decision 6, so your readers will affect what information you can convey and how you can convey it in a visual aid. People read visual aids in much the same way that they read text, with many of the same difficulties. You need to keep your visual aid readable by considering some of the same elements that keep text readable.

Is the form familiar?

Most readers are familiar with many different types of visual aids: photographs, simple bar charts and line graphs, pie charts, and even thermobar weather maps are used often in newspapers and in popular magazines like *Newsweek* and *Time*. As long as you keep these simple, you can feel fairly safe using them.

However, some technical fields have highly technical drawings that readers elsewhere in the organization may not be able to read easily. To include these visual aids in a report, you need to make sure that your readers will be able to read and understand them. Otherwise, your visual aid may work against your message. Of course, you could place these visual aids into an appendix with other technical information.

Is the design simple?

Basically, you want to keep the information simple and in a

form that the reader can understand quickly and easily. Make your visual aid user friendly, i.e. make it simple and easy to use. If you begin adding too many variables and pieces of information to the visual aid, you will overwhelm your reader with "visual junk." Try to keep clean lines, use lots of white space, and limit the number of pieces of information to about five different types.

Computer hacks (or people who have just gotten a PC desk top publishing program) can be the worst offenders here. Thrilled with what they can create at the touch of a key with various programs, they fill their graphics with too much information in too cluttered a design. (Woe to the person who also has access to "clip art.") As a report writer, you may not have access to all of the computer glitz now available for visual aids, but, with or without a computer, the advice is the same: Keep It Simple!

Are there cues to guide the reader?

Readers need signals about what's important, just as they need those cues in your text. The simplest place to give a cue is in the title. Since readers often skim a technical document, and you want them to get information from even the table of contents, you'll want to write good chapter titles too. But what makes a good title?

Good titles are both precise and concise. An informative title lets the reader know the kind of information that is available by reading the visual aid. Avoid titles that contain little information, such as

Table 1: Two Variables.

This title tells the reader nothing except that there are two variables. Look how much more informative a title like this one is to a reader:

Table 1: Comparisons of Wind and Rain

Readers want concise titles too. Avoid titles that are redundant or repetitious, such as

Table 1: Information about Survey Respondents

Instead, you could eliminate the "Information about" since we would expect that the table would contain information.

Is the visual aid efficient for the reader?

Like good prose, a good visual aid should convey its information without unnecessary effort on the part of the reader. In addition to the suggestions above, you can do three more things to keep your reader efficient.

☐ Review the visual aid as though you were the cold reader. Can you follow the information? Can you see what the parts are and the point of the visual aid?

☐ Introduce your visual aid in your prose. Don't let it sit in your text like a stranger with no introduction. Readers will wonder why it's there anyway, so anticipate the question. The last thing you want a reader to think about a visual aid is, "Why is this thing stuck in here?"

☐ Guide your reader to the visual aid. If it is not near the prose that introduces it, give a page number and always give the reader a cue, such as "As you can see from table I," or "See figure 1." You can always give the reference to the figure parenthetically, as in **(see figure 1)**.

Now that you have considered your reader, you must focus next on your purpose.

What Is My Purpose?

What you are trying to accomplish with your visual aid is one of the most important decisions you will make. You must know what you are trying to emphasize with the visual aid AND what you want the reader to do with the information you have provided. As you decide both of these points, you will be deciding the form of your visual aid. For example, suppose you are doing a report on a private school, the Windwood Academy. Let's say that you want to report the tuition costs over the past four years. You could show this information in a simple total cost chart:

Year	1986	1987	1988	1989
Tuition	$3,456	$4,453	$4,498	$5,684

Worried that parents would focus too much on the cost increases, you might want to temper this information with comparisons to other schools in the area. (See figure 2.)

Figure 2: Comparison of Tuition Costs and Increases

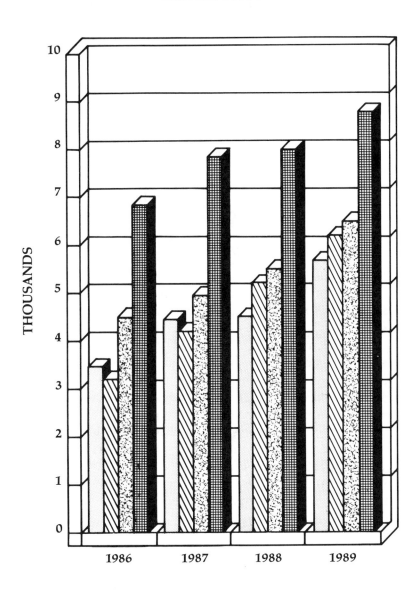

Windwood

Montgomery Academy

Ferguson Country Day

Colonial Friends

Or you might want to emphasize that tuition fails to cover all the costs of the school and use a pie chart to show what percentage of other monies are used to meet the school's costs. (See figure 3).

Figure 3: Sources of Income

1989

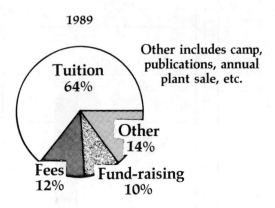

Other includes camp, publications, annual plant sale, etc.

As you can see, the point that you want the readers to take away from the visual aid will shape the type of visual aid that you use.

Finally, remember that visual aids can't do all the work. You must let the reader know what conclusions to draw from the data. Information never just sits there by itself. Readers will impart meaning if you don't give any of your own. So draw the conclusions that you want your visual aid to make.

Sometimes, you can let the graphics draw the conclusion. This chart from a *Washington Post* news article on the Baltimore Orioles baseball team is certainly ensuring that the reader understands that the Orioles did a lot better in 1989 than in 1988. Even so, the chart accompanied a feature article about the improved Orioles.

WRITING TO PLEASE YOUR BOSS

SO FAR, SO GOOD
Orioles team totals at the half

BATTING	1988	1989	% Chng.
Record	28-59	48-36	+71.4%
Average	.228	.260	+14.0%
On-base avg.	.302	.339	+12.3%
Runs	294	396	+34.7%
Hits	655	740	+13.0%
Doubles	109	139	+27.5%
Triples	10	24	+140%
Home runs	74	72	-2.7%
RBI	274	369	+34.7%
Walks	297	338	+12.8%
Strikeouts	462	464	+0.4%
Stolen bases	37	62	+67.6%
Caught stealing	24	24	0
Errors	63	40	-36.5%
PITCHING	1988	1989	% Chng.
ERA	4.73	3.81	+19.5%
Saves	14	27	+92.9%
Hits	849	779	-8.2%
Runs	449	335	-25.4%
Earned runs	400	319	-20.3%
Home runs	79	67	-15.2%
Walks	257	215	-16.3%
Strikeouts	406	343	-15.5%

July 12, 1989

Other times, you might need to make the point in your text and not in the graphics. Again, in the Windwood Academy report, you might say something like the following: "As you can see from the comparisons of tuitions with other schools, Windwood Academy remains moderately priced." Or you could say: "Despite the increases in tuition, the costs of running the school continue to outreach the tuition costs. We are relying increasingly on alternative sources of income in order to hold down tuition costs."

No matter how you decide to handle it, be sure that you tell the reader what to conclude from the table, chart, or other graphic.

Ethics and Graphics

For all writing, but especially for graphics, we must add a fourth element of concern: Have I misled the reader of the visual aid? Given the power of the visual image, as a writer you must be particularly careful that you have not unintentionally misled the readers of your visual aid. We've included in Value Added II an article that we feel will discuss more fully the concerns of misleading a reader—intentionally or not.

A Final Note

Chapter 8 lists several graphics packages that you might use on the job. Value Added I puts together a description of various kinds of data graphics that you might use and offers guidelines on using them. We've also included a listing of some books that will help you make decisions about when to use a particular visual aid and how to construct it.

The Decision Worksheets

Worksheet A provides a series of questions that will help trigger the use of graphics in your report.

Worksheet B helps you plan the graphic by considering purpose and audience.

Decision 11
Worksheet A: Finding Graphics

Instructions: Answer the following questions. Any question to which you answer "yes" is a potential graphic for your report.

Subject

Do I have a physical object that I could show?

Am I comparing one total with other totals?

Am I showing the relative importance of elements as components of a whole?

Am I showing the frequency of distribution over time or in a location?

Am I showing change over a period of time?

Am I showing the relative values of a variety of elements?

Am I indicating a complex process?

Am I including detailed information that I could put into a matrix for reference?

Do I have an important point that I could emphasize visually?

Source: Connie Drake Wilson, Instructional Systems Consultant, Wilson Associates, Washington, D.C.

Decision 11
Worksheet B: Planning Graphics

Instructions: Answer the following questions for each visual aid you are considering.

Purpose
What is the point that I want to make with this visual aid? What's the message that I'm trying to convey?

Audience
Who is the audience for this visual aid?

Is the type of graphic familiar to them?

Is the design simple?

Where do I need to include "cue" words for the audience?

How can I make the graphic efficient for the audience to read?

CHAPTER FIVE

Revising

You now have a rough cut. If you have followed the planning decisions rigorously, this draft should serve reasonably well. But no plan is perfect. Chances are that your planning decisions didn't anticipate all of the problems you would encounter in drafting. New information arises or the requirements of the organization change during the project. Or you might have focused less fully on some decisions than on others. So now you're revising.

In effect, the revising stage gives you the opportunity to rethink what you've written. The planning and drafting stages have allowed you to find out what you know. Now revising can allow you to convey what you know so that your readers also know it. This stage can be trickier than you might anticipate. Revising is much more than a mere matter of making corrections. You will need to return to your planning decisions to help you assess what you still need to do. After all, you're trying to get what's in your head into someone else's head—without a Vulcan mind meld.

You might think of it this way: planning and drafting are like the first two stages of a three-stage rocket. They get you off the ground and into the air. But it's the revising stage that gets you to the target. In the revising stage, you'll focus the draft to do two things: one, convey your message to your own satisfaction, and two, present your message in a form that is easy for the reader to use.

In an organization, revising generally occurs in two forms. First, you—and your team, if you collaborated—will work to shape up your rough draft. Next, you'll send it forward for a different kind of collaboration: the review process. Your manager—sometimes a string of managers—will work on it further. The object of this process is to focus your draft as fully as possible on fulfilling the writing situation.

Getting in Shape for Review

Because some revising decisions will be made by the reviewer, your task at this stage is to get the document ready for collaborating with the reviewer. You need to ensure that your essential theme is apparent, that your message comes through in your document; that's what a good reviewer will check for first. You want to make review as efficient as possible. The less you make the reviewer guess your intent or interpret your meaning, the closer you and your reviewer can come in cooperating on your document.

You have another reason for taking the initial stages of revising seriously. It's a sad but true fact that most organizations fail to account fully for the collaboration required between drafters and reviewers in the revising stage. This is the reason that the draft may come back to you for more work after you have been assigned a new project. Consequently, you need to do whatever you can at this stage to anticipate review concerns. The whole Decision Method, in fact, is aimed at helping you anticipate those concerns and generate a document to satisfy them. In a sense, you've already prepared for the review in the planning modules. If you have shared Decisions 1 through 8 with your manager, then neither of you should have any major surprises when you send the document forward.

Since your decisions in the planning stage identified the target and set the trajectory for your document, you will need to return to those decisions now. As you begin to revise, you can re-evaluate those decisions and determine the extent to which you have activated them in your draft.

This is where it gets personal. Each draft and each person will need attention in different places. When you're revising, you're checking to see that your purpose is fulfilled and that you've answered the questions your reader might have.

Module D:
Revising
(Decisions 12 through 14)

This module will help you prepare your document for review.

Decision 12
Is My Structure Apparent
to My Reader?

Having your theme or message present in your document is not the same as having it easily recognized by and apparent to a reader. And, since you are trying to ensure that review will be as efficient as possible, you want to make sure that what your reviewers understand as your main point *is* what you intended them to understand. In this decision, you'll focus on using different techniques to underscore your main point.

What Do Readers Read?

Consider your own experience. Do you read everything that comes across your desk? Or do you skim?

Executive readers often preview a document by reading first the title, then the executive summary, the first paragraph in each section, and the headings. They're looking for a sense of the big picture before they go back to fill in the detail. They need to know the basic story and how much it affects them before they commit their time to your document. If they can't easily follow the structure, your document will end up at the bottom of the In basket.

Other readers, even those with the greatest need for your technical details, will also skim for what they need. They will want to locate the information they need, and will need to understand the context in which it operates.

What holds for the end users of your document also holds for your reviewer. A reviewer who can't easily see your basic message in a first reading may well develop misconceptions about your intent. Several problems can occur as a result, depending on the skill of the reviewer. One, a reviewer who doesn't perceive your message immediately may put off conducting the review, causing delays for you and even more time pressure when the draft does come back. Two, the reviewer may miss your point, and address review comments to a misperceived message. And three, the reviewer may develop a negative sense of your capabilities as a writer.

Structured Reading

To revise efficiently, you need to simulate the way a sophisticated reader will approach your document. A technique called structured reading can help you simulate this approach. Structured reading lets you start with the big issues and check out whether you're on the mark with each one. You work on revising according to priorities, dealing first with your overall structure, then with paragraph issues, and finally with sentences.

Why does it work? Well, for one thing, it keeps you from wasting your revision efforts. Most people do a first reading of a draft with a pencil in hand, making corrections as they read. But what happens if the draft requires big changes in its structure? Then all these fine-tuning changes may well be lost.

The other reason that structured reading works is that it can enhance the reception your document gets from your reader. It does so by calling your attention to the guideposts for reading that your reader will respond to, consciously or unconsciously. These guideposts are called **advance organizers**, and they help the reader skim by underscoring your important points. They are like the advance staff in a political campaign, who ensure that the candidate is in the right place at the right time. Advance organizers in your writing ensure that your points have visibility for the people who count—your readers.

In the workplace, it's safe to assume that your readers are busy. Advance organizers focus their attention efficiently, on the assumption that it's what's up front that counts.

Let's see how much you can learn by reading only advance organizers. Below are the advance organizers from two chapters of a forty-five-page government report, deliberately chosen for the obscurity of its subject, "value engineering." Chances are you're unfamiliar with this term. See how much you can come to understand about it simply by doing the first phase of a structured reading: reading for advance organizers.

First the opening to chapter one, the Introduction. It tells you the definition of value engineering.

What is Value Engineering?

Value engineering is the scientific method of analyzing and redesigning a product or service so that its function can be achieved at the lowest possible overall cost. The product or service may be redesigned by using different materials, by applying new technology or a more efficient production or delivery process, or by eliminating unnecessary components. A tenet of value engineering is that, while anything less than essential functional capability is unacceptable, anything more is wasteful and should be eliminated.

Value engineering can be applied during any phase of a project from inception to completion. However, in many cases it is applied to a product or service design that has been firmly established. Thus value engineering may be viewed as the "auditing arm" of engineering.

Now read ONLY the headings for the rest of the chapter.

☐ VALUE ENGINEERING IS A RECOGNIZED TOOL FOR REDUCING COST AND INCREASING PRODUCTIVITY

☐ WE HAVE A LONGSTANDING INTEREST IN VALUE ENGINEERING

☐ OBJECTIVES, SCOPE AND METHODOLOGY

No surprises here. This is a standard introduction chapter, defining the subject, demonstrating the writer's stance, and confirming the research approach.

Now let's use the same techniques for chapter two. First, the chapter title and the introductory paragraph.

> **Management Emphasis on Contractor Program has Increased Savings Some But Not Enough**
>
> The Department of Defense, the Army, and the Air Force have recently acted to strengthen their value engineering programs, paying particular attention to the contractor component. Management actions have led to revised policies and guidance, an overall VECP savings goal, and more effective correspondence encouraging contractors to participate in the value engineering program. The Air Force program was reorganized and a DOD awards program was introduced. DOD reported total savings for the fiscal year 1982 contractor program of $144.7 million—an increase of about $50 million over fiscal year 1981 but still more than $300 million short of DOD's established goal of $448.7 million. The Navy, which has put less management emphasis on value engineering than the Army and Air Force, has achieved lower savings than those two services.

What have we learned? We know the players and the amounts involved.

Next the headings for chapter two. They tell us the major players and their relative standings.

DOD HAS PUT MORE MANAGEMENT EMPHASIS ON THE CONTRACTOR PROGRAM, BUT NAVY LAGS BEHIND

Army, with longstanding support for value engineering, is improving its program

Air Force emphasizes contractor component in its value engineering program

Navy has placed less management emphasis on its value engineering program

CONTRACTOR COMPONENT SAVINGS HAVE IN-CREASED BUT COULD BE GREATER

Reported savings have increased: Each military service has had successful VECPs

What do the reported savings represent?

DOD has not met its own goal for savings

Most major weapons systems have not reported VECP savings

Look at the graphics. They give us comparisons of the relative savings over time. In fact, they reinforce some of the actual dollar amounts we read in the introductory paragraph.

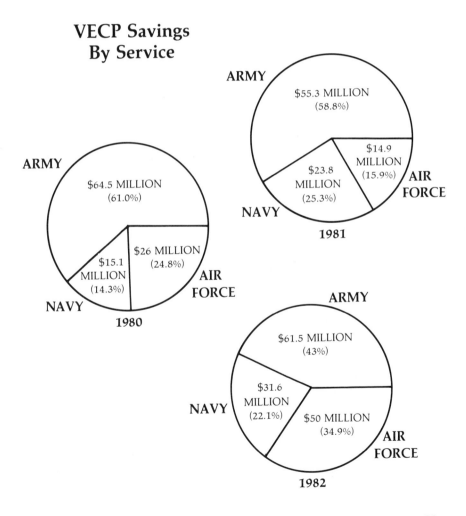

VECP Savings
By Service

ARMY
$55.3 MILLION
(58.8%)

$14.9 MILLION
(15.9%) AIR FORCE

$23.8 MILLION
(25.3%)

NAVY

1981

ARMY
$64.5 MILLION
(61.0%)

$26 MILLION
(24.8%)

$15.1 MILLION
(14.3%)

NAVY

AIR FORCE

1980

ARMY
$61.5 MILLION
(43%)

$31.6 MILLION
(22.1%)

$50 MILLION
(34.9%)

NAVY

AIR FORCE

1982

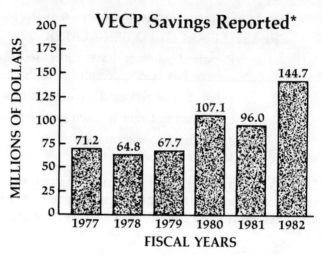

VECP Savings Reported*

MILLIONS OF DOLLARS

FISCAL YEARS

* Includes three military services and Defense Logistics Agency.

Now look at the section on the Army, the top performer. Reading only the first sentence in each paragraph will tell you why the Army is so successful.

☐ The well-established Army value-engineering program, which has benefited from significant management support in the past, recently increased its emphasis on the contractor component of the program.

☐ The Army has an effective structure for managing its total value engineering program and has assigned more full-time staff to the program than the other two services.

☐ Army headquarters and several major commands recently directed that the program be improved and assigned VECP savings goals to subordinate commands and selected weapon system program managers.

☐ One unique characteristic that appears to strengthen the Army program is the longstanding practice of setting both dollar and numerical VECP goals.

☐ Major Army commands have also pursued other alternatives for encouraging contractor involvement and increasing VECP savings.

☐ In its efforts to encourage contractors, the Army has also successfully tested an experimental value-engineering clause.

That's as far as we're going to go. You need read no further to know the essential points of this report. While you have gained little specific information, you have gained a broad overview of the subject. You now know enough to ask intelligent questions —in fact, you now know enough to read the report with greater comprehension and retention.

You can see the value of advance organizers for establishing your key points and giving your reader easy access to them. Your first step, then, in revising your own draft is to check for your advance organizers and put them in place if they're not there.

What Are Advance Organizers?

Advance organizers come in several forms, including executive summaries, introductory statements, headings, subheadings, topic sentences, and typographic arrangements.

Executive Summaries. Summary sections placed at the beginning of a document help to orient readers to what follows. Executive summaries should be complete and independent of the report, allowing a busy executive to skip the rest of the report yet still get the essential information from it. Even in a memo, a short one- or two-sentence overview will serve the same function as an executive summary. Reviewers, and the many other readers who will read the rest of the report, use the executive summary to tell them what to expect.

Topic Sentences. Topic sentences forecast for the reader the information that a paragraph will contain, and transitions guide the readers through the logic of a paragraph. (We'll talk about topic sentences in the next decision.)

Headings. Sidecaps (such as **What Are Advance Organizers?**), as well as other headings, show the reader the major sections of the report. Headings help a reader to locate needed information, and they make visible the organization and message of the document. By reading only the headings, reviewers should have a sense of the organization of the report and its important points. (For documents that have the general public as a primary reader, use headings phrased as questions to help the reader find needed information. Generic headings, like **Introduction,** seem to be the least helpful to readers.)

Headings can be in the form of summary statements. You

will use them to emphasize the major theme behind a section. They are usually of two types: **phrases** or **complete sentences**. Before reviewers begin to read a section, they know what they will be reading about and why.

Introductory Statements. These are often relatively short paragraphs or sections that provide an overview of the section.

Numbers. At the sentence level, you can cue your reviewer about what is to come with a very simple addition. Instead of stating that "several themes emerged," you can say that "seven" themes emerged.

Using Guide Words. You can help your reviewer stay focused by providing place markers, like "first," "second," "next," and so on. These words remind readers where they are in the document and the message. You use transitional words in the same way to mark the path of your logic. (We'll talk a bit more about this in the next decision also.)

Making the Reader See. One other important aspect to consider as you revise for a reviewer is the arrangement of words on the page. What you place in bold, what you break out in a list, what you surround with white space—all of these tell your reviewer what you want to emphasize and what you want to call attention to. As you might expect, items to which you choose to give typographical or graphic emphasis should be important.

Typographic Arrangement. You can use listings to help readers know when items are important and are of equal or similar importance. Generally, you mark these listings with a bullet or asterisk. For example, which of these passages is easier to read?

Passage 1. The eight missing file records were examined against printouts to determine whether any documented data were not in the database. The following updates were encoded: two violation-type modifications, one termination date, one modification to scheduled abatement date, one vacation notice, one telephone number modification, two service dates.

Passage 2. The eight missing file records were examined against printouts to determine whether any documented data were not in the database. The following updates were encoded:

two violation-type modifications,

one termination date,

one modification to scheduled abatement date,

one vacation notice,

one telephone number modification,

two service dates.

You can see at a glance that the second passage will be easier to comprehend and retain. White space, indentations, even paragraphing make a document seem more accessible.

Consider which of these documents you would rather read, or which one would be easier to find information in.

Highlighting Techniques.   Boldface type and capitalization are two aspects of typographic arrangement that help readers know where to focus their attention. You have to use a light hand here, however; if you boldface and capitalize everything, your reader's attention still can't focus. Also be careful about putting long blocks of prose into all capitals; they tend to be harder to read than a combination of upper and lower case.

Scenario

Let's look at advance organizers in the review process. You are a consultant for a marketing firm that is preparing a report on marketing suggestions for Windwood Academy, a small, independent school. As part of your data gathering, you surveyed the parents about the strengths and weaknesses of the school. Although your report will eventually go to the Board of Trustees of the school, you are now concerned with your immediate supervisor. You know that she will read your draft and she has complained that it takes her too long to find the bottom line in your reports. You know you have your basic message clear, but you decide to read through your report one more time before sending it up to your supervisor to ensure that she can get to the bottom line quickly.

A Portion of Draft 1

In our survey, the Windwood Academy's philosophy was repeatedly mentioned by parents. Parents specifically cited the school's philosophy as its strength, and, through their other responses, touched on several aspects of the school's philosophy: such as the values placed on the individual; helping children grow in self-confidence, self-respect, and tolerance for others; the nurturing environment; a flexible, well-rounded curriculum; and the happy environment as well as other aspects of a progressive philosophy, such as attention to learning styles, emphasis on problem solving and independent thinking, and so on.

Parents described the faculty as of high quality, caring and interested, warm, recognizing and valuing individual differences, and providing personal attention to the child.

Parents suggested that more after-school activities, especially sports, be added to the school. They also requested a strengthening of academics, especially in foreign languages, computers, and music. They also wanted an increase in racial, ethnic, and socioeconomic diversity.

Well, you decide, it's not impossible to read, but neither is it very easy to skim. You decide to revise using advance organizers to highlight your message for your supervisor. The information is basically the same, but you try to help her *see* the important points through typographic arrangement and through other advance organizers. After you have revised, your report reads like this:

What Did We Find From the Survey?

Parent responses about current strengths and suggested changes grouped into a total of five themes.

Under current strengths, two major themes emerged:
- [ ] the philosophy of the school, and
- [ ] the excellence of the faculty.

Under suggested changes, three themes emerged:
- [ ] adding after-school activities, especially sports;
- [ ] strengthening academics in particular areas such as foreign language, computers, and music; and,
- [ ] increasing racial, ethnic, socioeconomic diversity.

What Themes Should a Marketing Campaign Emphasize?

The two strengths identified by parents seem the logical choices for the thrust of an immediate marketing campaign. Parents felt strongly about these points and indicated that they were the reasons that they had chosen the school. The specifics within each of these themes would provide excellent marketing points to the targeted communities.

The Progressive Philosophy Is a Major Strength.
Windwood Academy's progressive philosophy was the dominant theme. Parents specifically cited the school's philosophy as its strength, and, through their other responses, touched on several aspects of the progressive philosophy:

value placed on the individual;

helping children grow in self-confidence, self-respect, and tolerance for others;

nurturing environment;

flexible, well-rounded curriculum; and

a happy environment.

> Parents were also pleased with other aspects of a progressive philosophy, such as attention to learning styles and an emphasis on problem-solving and independent thinking.
>
> **The Faculty Is a Major Strength.**
> The quality of the Windwood Academy faculty was the second major theme. Parents saw the faculty as inextricably linked to the success of the school's philosophy, and many of the other strengths listed for Windwood Academy could exist only in the presence of a strong faculty. Parents characterized the faculty in a number of ways:
>
> > having high quality,
> >
> > caring and interested,
> >
> > having warmth,
> >
> > recognizing and valuing individual differences, and
> >
> > providing personal attention to the child.

As you read through your rewrite, you feel that you have highlighted the points of this report so that your supervisor will have quick and easy access to them. In addition, you're surprised to find that as you tried to make your points clearer for her, your points became clearer for you too.

What you've discovered is another advantage of revising. Revising—like any other part of the writing process—is recursive. As you reconsider your draft, you will constantly cycle between your reader's needs and your own needs, between your reader's need to read and understand easily and your own need to work out exactly what you wanted to say. Getting your draft ready for review will often result in fine tuning of your basic message.

What About Readers Beyond the Reviewer?

Most documents have lives beyond the reviewer. Deciding how to make your draft easier to read for only the reviewer can be short-sighted, especially if you know that the document will have multiple readers with varying levels of expertise. In such a situation, advance organizers are essential. Advance organizers allow readers to develop an overall sense of your message quickly, and sort out what (or even whether) they need to read. Apart from reviewers, few readers will read every word of a large document. Advance organizers allow readers to focus attention where they need to. Policy makers are likely to focus on the executive summary as a way of determining how to delegate responsibility. Experts or specialists will use the advance organizers to find the data they are interested in. Where material is technical, advance organizers help the non-specialist reader put it in context; where large amounts of data are involved, advance organizers allow readers to focus on the big picture.

It's a rule of thumb that the more work you put into the writing, the less work the reader has to put into the reading. Before you start to reflect on the general unfairness of it all, consider this: your highest-level readers may not be able to afford more than a ten- or fifteen-minute reading of your document. In such a case, your advance organizers will have to carry your message—or it may not get across to a crucial reader at all.

Decision 12
Worksheet

To check for advance organizers, capitalize on the outline you worked on in Decisions 5 through 8.

1. Do my major points in the outline occupy positions of major visibility?
2. Have I provided an executive summary, if possible?
3. Does my title indicate the major theme of my report?
4. Have I used headings and subheadings to mark major sections of the report?
5. Have I used summary statements as overviews to forecast information for my reader?
6. Have I used topic sentences to guide my reader through a paragraph?
7. Have I used guide words or transitions to help a reader predict the points of my document?
8. Have I used typographic arrangement to emphasize my main points?
9. Have I used highlighting techniques to emphasize my points?
10. Have I overused typographic arrangement or highlighting techniques?
11. Have I used graphics to emphasize important points?

Decision 13
How Can My Paragraphs Emphasize My Purpose for the Reader?

You've looked at overall structure in Decision 12 to determine how well it serves your readers' needs. This decision will look at how well your internal paragraph structure reinforces your purpose. You will consider **topic sentences, grouping of information**, and **transitions**. As you work on revising, these techniques will help you shape your paragraphs and nail down your message.

Remember, you may not need to consider all of these aspects for every draft. Some drafts may need a bit of work on topic sentences, and other drafts may need attention to grouping of information. The point is that until these are addressed, there's no point in trying to fix sentences. We'll do that in the next decision.

Topic Sentences

If you're doing a detailed revision, the first thing you need to look at in each paragraph is your topic sentence. The topic sentence in informative or analytic writing will usually come first, to get the reader ready for the information that follows it. Not every paragraph in every document you write will necessarily start with—or even have—a topic sentence. But the more complex your information is, the more you need topic sentences to keep it straight for the reader.

Topic sentences do two things: announce the **subject** of the paragraph, and give that subject a spin, or **controlling idea**. These two elements interact to make up your major statement for the paragraph, usually in the form of a generalization, or overview.

You can think of the relationship between subject and controlling idea in several ways. The subject names the point of departure; the controlling idea names the direction of movement. The subject tells *what* we're talking about or the matter we're concerned with; the controlling idea tells *why* we're concerned with it or the significance of the matter. The subject ties us into the general context or the old information. (It may be the same as the subject of the previous paragraph, or even the whole document.) The controlling idea, on the other hand, ties us into the development of this particular paragraph or the new information. It cues the reader about how to perceive the more specific sentences—usually containing pieces of new information—that follow.

Take a look at the following topic sentence:

☐ FAA needs to improve its procedures for identifying pilots who may jeopardize flight safety through alcohol use.

The subject, or point of departure, is FAA or Federal Aviation Administration. (In fact, the subject of the topic sentence should announce the subject of the paragraph.) The controlling idea, or direction of movement for this paragraph, is the need to improve procedures for identifying alcohol use. (The controlling idea should be a word or phrase that follows and says something about the subject.) Together, the subject and controlling idea enable the topic sentence to set the reader's expectations. They should generate the context for the information that follows, and may characterize it.

What do you expect the rest of the sentences in the example paragraph to do? According to the topic sentence, it will discuss what FAA does—or doesn't—do to identify alcohol use in pilots. You can expect some specific procedures. Here is the rest of the paragraph:

☐ At present, the agency does not routinely check the pilots' state traffic conviction records for alcohol-related motor vehicle convictions. In addition, while FAA requests pilots to disclose these convictions in their medical histories, the pilots often conceal this information. Finally, FAA has not provided in its pilot medical examination guidelines any criteria for diagnosing alcoholism.

Does this paragraph fulfill your expectations? Yes, since each sentence says something the FAA does or does not do. The paragraph gives three specific procedures the agency needs to improve: checking for traffic convictions, requesting medical histories, and providing criteria for diagnosing alcoholism.

Grouping Similar Information

A second technique that you can use to ensure that your paragraphs are helping your reader is to group similar information within a paragraph. In order to give the reader a coherent picture, you also need to group your information in such a way that the reader can follow it. Look at the sample paragraph below. Before it can make sense to a reader (and, perhaps, before the writer can hope to compose a topic sentence), the information will have to be regrouped.

☐ The store equipment was appraised at $7,349 low to $10,532 high value. The high bidder was Frank Gurlin of Gurlin Enterprises with a bid of $6,394. This bid is 85 percent of low appraisal. The canned goods stock was appraised at $1,475.50 low to $1,942.75 high value. The high bidder was High Mesa Ranch Supply, Inc., with a bid of $779. This bid is 52 percent of low appraisal. We ran an ad for three weeks in four different newspapers. The property is in the downtown industrial area with little night activity, subject to vandalism and thievery. We received five bids on the equipment, ranging from $6,394 to $3,209. The two bids received on the food were $390 and $779. A schedule of the bids is attached.

Consider what different groupings are present. (You might want to get out your Post-it ™ notes again to do this kind of rewriting, or use different colored markers.) The paragraph includes information about the two kinds of property: equipment and stock. These things, in turn, have been the subject of bidding and appraisal.

equipment
 bids
  five bids received
  low bid $3,209
  high bid $6,394
  high bidder Frank Gurlin of Gurlin Enterprises
 appraisal
  $7,349 low
  $10,532 high
  high bid is 85 percent of low appraisal

canned goods stock

>bids

>>two bids received

>>low bid $390

>>high bid $779

>>high bidder High Mesa Ranch Supply, Inc.

>appraisal

>>$1,475.50 low

>>$1,942.75 high

>>high bid is 52 percent of low appraisal

miscellaneous

>We ran an ad for three weeks in four different newspapers.

>The store is in downtown industrial area with little night activity, subject to vandalism and thievery.

>A schedule of the bids is attached.

For this paragraph to make sense—either to the writer or to a reader—similar information needs to be grouped together: information about equipment together and information about the stock together, with bids and appraisals appropriately grouped for each category. Two pieces of miscellaneous information are background, and probably belong in a preceding paragraph.

Revised for a reader, this paragraph might well read as two:

☐ We tried to avoid continued exposure of the property, which is in a downtown industrial area with little night activity, subject to vandalism and thievery. To dispose of the property, we advertised for three weeks in four papers.

☐ Finally, we accepted bids lower than the appraised value. For the equipment, we received five bids, with a low bid of $3,209 and a high of $6,394. High bidder was Frank Gurlin of Gurlin Enterprises, whose bid represented 85 percent of the low value appraisal of $7,349. High value appraisal was $10,532. For the food stock, we received two bids, with a low of $390 and a high of $779. High bidder was High Mesa Food Supply, Inc., with a bid of 52 percent of the

$1,475.50 low value appraisal. High value appraisal was $1,942.75. A schedule of bids is attached.

The writer of the first draft may well have been focused on trying to remember the facts—putting them down as they came to memory. The second draft needed to supply a reason for the reader to process the facts, and a method for doing so. The topic sentence and regrouping of facts accomplished this purpose.

Transitions

Once you have written a topic sentence to cue what you're talking about, you will need to use the third paragraph technique—**transitions**—to keep the reader's attention on track. To show how transitions function, we've removed the transitions from the following paragraph:

☐ The FBI wants to protect itself from charges that it is investigating purely political activities. In its investigations of groups who field political candidates, such as the Socialist Workers Party and the National Caucus of Labor Committees, the FBI has directed that political candidates not be actively investigated. FBI agents should not solicit or actively seek information by taking actions on their own, such as a physical surveillance, which would result in obtaining information. Headquarters advised the field officers that these individuals' activities may be followed through confidential sources who volunteer information and through public information.

Here is the paragraph with the transitions included in boldface type:

☐ The FBI wants to protect itself from charges that it is investigating purely political activities. **Thus,** in its investigations of groups who field political candidates, such as the Socialist Workers Party and the National Caucus of Labor Committees, the FBI has directed that political candidates not be actively investigated. **That is,** FBI agents should not solicit or actively seek information by taking actions on their own, such as a physical surveillance, which would result in obtaining information. **However,** headquarters

WRITING TO PLEASE YOUR BOSS

advised the field officers that these individuals' activities may be followed through confidential sources who volunteer information and through public information.

You might note a difference in the way you perceive the information in the paragraph now. For instance, did you realize on reading the first paragraph that the last sentence gives an exception? It tells the one thing the FBI *can* do, while the rest of the paragraph focuses on what it can't.

Transitions help readers follow your line of thought. Much as highway signs give a driver advance warning of what exits are coming up, transitions help the reader know what new directions your thought is taking. They let your reader see the relationship of one sentence to another. You might want to remember this simple rule of thumb: if you have an idea contrasted with something previous (like an exception), you *must* use a transition to mark the contrast. In other cases, you have more leeway.

Here's a list of common transitional words and the kinds of guidance they give a reader.

Common Transitions

Cause and Effect

because	as a result
since	therefore
as	consequently
for	thus
due to	accordingly
owing to	on account of

Addition

and
also
too
as well as
besides
including
in addition
moreover
furthermore

Contrast

but
however
instead
yet
despite
otherwise
nevertheless
except for
in spite of

Comparison

similarly
likewise
in the same way
just as . . . so

Illustration

for example
specifically
for instance
in other words
that is

Sequence

first
next
after
ultimately
before
finally

Time

now
then
later
currently
meanwhile
earlier

Place

here
there
at this point
below
next to
in front of
alongside

Condition

if
even if
although
unless
supposing that
given that
assuming that

Duration

to some extent
to some degree
to date
up to now
so far
until

Paragraphs and Purpose

After a structured reading, take a more systematic look at your purpose. Review your Decision 1 worksheet. Has your sense of purpose changed since you articulated your communication purpose at the beginning of the assignment? Have you fulfilled your technical purpose as originally articulated?

Scenario

Let's look at the role your original purpose can play as you revise. You are the team leader for a government project on preventing high school dropouts. You are working on a position paper for the head of your agency about the problems of collecting national data, and have just prepared a rough draft of the executive summary. You have read the draft through once, and you're a little uneasy about it, without being able to pinpoint why. Before you pass it up the line to a project director, you ask a colleague, a friend of yours, to take a look at it. You're out of the office when she pops in to return it, so she leaves the following note stuck to it: "Wow! I thought you were *for* this program."

You're irritated by your friend's comment, because in fact you *are* in favor of the program you're reporting on. You mutter to yourself, "What's the matter; can't she read?" And you set out to find all the places in the draft that show you support the program. You go through the draft and mark all the positive statements with a plus, all the negative ones with a minus. Here is the draft:

Original Version

OVERALL CONCLUSIONS AND MATTERS FOR CONGRESSIONAL CONSIDERATION

With some limitations, the cooperative approach can be a viable way of collecting national data on dropout-prevention programs for congressional and federal agency oversight purposes in a timely manner with reduced levels of burden. An inherent limitation of this approach is that data reported by some states will not always be comparable with that from others, as we found in the twenty state programs we examined in-depth. Nevertheless, many state officials want to make this approach work because they see the importance of providing national level data to the Congress for continued support of dropout-prevention programs and they like the flexibility this approach provides.

Our review of the twenty sets of data identified several appropriate and inappropriate uses of data collected under this approach, and several that should be limited. This approach can be an effective way of collecting data for oversight, technical assistance, information exchange, and tracking national trends in funding and services. Furthermore, it promotes interstate cooperation by involving state officials in the design and implementation of the system.

However, it may not be appropriate to use data collected under this approach to allocate federal funds, determine the magnitude of needs between individual states, or compare program effectiveness among states. At the national level, sufficient procedures are not in place to verify that data reported are reasonably accurate. Consequently, if these data were used to allocate funds, some states may have an incentive to report data that will advance their interests.

Furthermore, the usefulness of these data is limited in making state-by-state comparisons, such as the number of clients served, the types of services provided, and total dollars spent. Such comparisons highlight weaknesses in differences in definitions of these categories by states. For example, comparing the cost per client served (i.e., dropout-prone or "high risk" students) would be invalid because of differences in state cost accounting procedures.

Additionally, this approach may not be effective if the data alone are to be used for monitoring state compliance with federal laws and regulations. In the absence of federal quality controls and monitoring, these data may not be adequate to judge whether a particular state is complying with federal laws and regulations; therefore, they should not be used as a basis for any decision concerning compliance issues. The data might, however, serve as a catalyst to determine if an audit should be undertaken.

A quick count of the positive and negative statements reveals that the negatives win out. Although you start out with a positive, your first two paragraphs actually follow a pattern of alternating positive and negative statements. And the last three paragraphs consist almost entirely of negative statements—your reservations about the program. These are followed by one last sentence that makes a positive statement.

Surprised by the results of this quick analysis, you think back to the writing situation as you conceived it at the beginning of the project. You've written about collecting data on high school dropouts for the head of the agency, who knows little about the technical aspects of data collection. You think you've done a good job in the executive summary of steering clear of technical language. And your role as writer, you originally figured, was to be the objective expert. You've bent over backwards to appear objective, telling both sides of the story. You think back to the purpose, as you initially conceived of it: to evaluate whether the cooperative approach is a viable way to obtain national data. You're puzzled. Haven't you done that?

You find the last issue a sticking point—the whole idea of the project was to evaluate the cooperative approach. And then you realize the problem: evaluation was your technical purpose. You had to perform an evaluation to answer the original question, "Is the cooperative approach a good idea?" In fact, now that you've done your technical evaluation, you know that the cooperative approach *is* a good idea (with some limitations), and you need to communicate that. In other words, your communication purpose is to endorse the program and recommend changes to improve it.

You realize you haven't done that yet. The draft represents a sort of thinking out loud, as you weighed the positive and negative points in your own mind. You have to admit it: you didn't really outline. A topic outline was all you put together. It was useful for you to use this draft to sort things out, and get them down on paper. But if a reader is going to see the issues the way you see them, you'll have to refocus to take the reader into account.

You rewrite the draft, this time with the idea of communicating the results of your evaluation. You focus on grouping information around topic sentences in line with your purpose, and getting to recommendations. Here is the revision:

Revision

OVERALL ASSESSMENT OF THE VIABILITY
OF THE COOPERATIVE APPROACH

The cooperative approach can be a viable way for federal policy-makers to obtain national dropout-prevention data on funding, services, and client characteristics. This approach allows states flexibility to accommodate national reporting requests by using their own information systems. It thereby reduces administrative burdens. Further, it promotes broad state cooperation by involving states in the design of national data collection and reporting systems.

However, because data collected by this approach are hard to compare, national leadership is needed to facilitate uniform state data collection to the extent possible. Unfortunately, the cooperative approach is not a viable way to obtain national data for other potential congressional and federal agency needs, such as allocating federal funds or determining state compliance with federal laws and regulations. In these cases, more comparable data are needed to minimize inequities in the results.

Where federal policy makers conclude that their data needs can be met through the cooperative approach, we have identified several factors that can enhance the viability of this approach. These include four program characteristics that made it easier to collect data through voluntary reporting: (1) there was a narrow scope of allowable activities, (2) federal funds were the primary source of program funding, (3) states had been involved in prior categorical grant programs, and (4) state governments had clear statutory authority to collect data from their localities.

In those dropout-prevention programs where the cooperative approach can be viable, we have identified six conditions that can increase data comparability: (1) national leadership in directing the development of model criteria and standardized forms, by either a federal agency or a national association; (2) states' recognition of the need for dropout-prevention data; (3) federal funding to support data collection activities; (4) designated national-level staff to work with state officials; (5) state officials' involvement in the design of the systems; and (6) federal statutes to encourage cooperation in data collection.

You're much happier with the second version—and grateful that your friend's remark made you review your planning documents and revise the draft before you sent it up for review. Even though it still sounds a bit bureaucratic, you decide to leave well enough alone for now, although you realize you might still want to polish it a bit more tomorrow. While it seems to lack a sense of urgency, at least now it says what you mean. The next decision will help you revise your sentences to focus more on the actions you're recommending.

Decision 13
Worksheet

Instructions: Answer the following questions for a draft of your own document.

1. What is my communication purpose?
2. What theme or message emerges when I read the topic sentences of the document?
3. Have I grouped similar information within a paragraph?
4. Have I used transitions to guide my reader through the logic of a paragraph?

Decision 14
How Can I Make My
Sentences Help My Reader?

Do you remember those long car trips, punctuated by "Are we there yet?" You may feel that way about your draft by now; in fact, although you may want to get rid of the draft as quickly as possible, it's probably worth your while to do one last run-through *before* you give it to your reviewer.

In drafting, you have focused on getting your information and ideas down on paper. In revising, so far you have checked to see that your message or theme is present in your report, and you have checked to see that your advance organizers give your reader easy access to your message. Decision 14 will help you remove major roadblocks to your message that might occur at the sentence level.

Since you have limited time for further revision, you'll need to focus your efforts where they really count. You can achieve this focus by checking for three sentence-level problems: inappropriate sentence length, frozen action, and buried sentence core.

Inappropriate Sentence Length

Since you probably don't have time to revise every sentence you write, you can use sentence length to help you decide what sentences to focus on. The length of the sentence is a symptom; like a fever, it tells you *something* is wrong, but it doesn't necessarily specify *what* is wrong. Nonetheless, you can treat the symptom and, in most cases, alleviate the problem. In general, very long and very short sentences tend to have more potential problems, and it is on these sentences that you should focus your attention.

How Long Is Long?

No sentence length is the ideal length. Some research[1] has suggested the following relationship between sentence length and reading ease:

---

[1]Rudolph Flesch, *The Art of Plain Talk* (New York: Harper and Brothers, 1946) cited in Kenneth W. Houp and Thomas E. Pearsall, *Reporting Technical Information* (New York: Macmillan Publishing Company, 1984), p.173.

very easy	8 words or fewer
easy	12
fairly easy	14
standard	17
fairly difficult	20
difficult	25
very difficult	29 words or more

Obviously, who your reader is will determine where your sentences can fall on this scale. A well-educated computer engineer reading difficult but familiar material on local area networking can probably deal with fairly long sentences. This same computer engineer reading difficult but unfamiliar material about genetic engineering would probably find the going easier with shorter sentences. Some rules of thumb: generally, keep sentences under 30 words. For professional reports, 17 to 25 words is considered standard sentence length. For material intended for the general public, 12 to 20 words is probably safer.

A Word on Short Sentences

Too short? Can a sentence be too short? True—short sentences can be very effective. They give a lot of emphasis to what they contain. Think of what you use short sentences for: "Thank you." "Sit down." "Get lost." "Go away." "Leave me alone."

A single short sentence can be a powerful way of emphasizing a point in a report. The short sentence tends to get high attention from a reader just by virtue of its being short.

But overusing short sentences can be dangerous. A series of very short sentences can be quite difficult to read, especially in instructions. Your sentences need to be long enough to group your information into units that seem logical to the reader. And if you are dealing with a politically delicate situation, where tact is important, a series of short sentences can come across like blows to the face.

Because of all the attention a short sentence attracts, make sure that your short sentences contain points you want emphasized.

How to Do It

Since you're pressed for time, looking for the sentences that are more likely to have problems narrows your task. You could count the words in all your sentences and graph them, but you can also try to get a visual sense of where the extremes of length occur.

Skim quickly down the right-hand margin. Generally, you want to come back to sentences that run more than three lines of typescript or less than half a line. (Look for the extra white space that occurs after the period.) Count the words in several sentences in a passage to get a feel for the sentence length you tend to use. Look at the chart. Consider your purpose, reader, writer's role, and subject to decide whether your sentences are too long. Consider the importance of your point to decide whether your sentences are too short.

Scenario

You've just finished drafting a report that recommends a design change for producing a one-way clutch assembly. You're fairly happy with most of the report, but this section about the new design costs is bothering you:

☐ Over the life of the project, the company would realize a substantial cost savings by adopting the proposed design for the one-way clutch assembly of the automatic overdrive transmission. This savings would be a total of $153,294. The total cost increase to the project would be $631,610, and this cost increase includes the increased cost per unit to have the race manufactured by an outside vendor, such as Integrity Plus Metal, and it includes the one-time cost for producing a new die of $12,250 by outside sources. It was found that producing the new powdered metal race in-house would be much too cost prohibitive due primarily to the additional equipment that would have to be purchased. There would be no additional labor activities involved in the assembly process, so no additional costs would be realized here.

☐ These initial increases in cost would be recovered over the life of the project due to the elimination of the pins required in the current assembly process. This represents a total savings of $270,970. The new design would eliminate the breakdowns, thus eliminating the repair costs of at least $53 per damaged unit. This would be a total additional savings of $512,934.

Because you can't put your finger on what's wrong, you decide to do a word count and graph the sentence lengths. Here are the results.

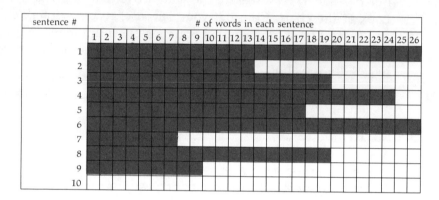

You look first at the short sentences. Do they need to have the additional emphasis that very short sentences give? When you look at the short sentences, you notice that each contains the same type of information:

☐ This savings would be a total of $153,294.
☐ This represents a total savings of $270,970.
☐ This would be a total additional savings of $512,934.

You ask yourself if this information should be emphasized and answer a resounding "Yes!" You decide to leave these short sentences for emphasis.

Next you look at the one other sentence that sticks out on your graph—the very long third sentence with 50 words.

☐ The total cost increase to the project would be $631,610, and this cost increase includes the increased cost per unit to have the race manufactured by an outside vendor, such as Integrity Plus Metal, and it includes the one-time cost for producing a new die of $12,250 by outside sources.

As you reread it, you realize that you have simply jammed too much information into one sentence. You decide to break the sentence up into two or three shorter sentences.

☐ The total cost increase to the project would be $631,610. This cost increase includes the increased cost per unit to have the race manufactured by an outside vendor, such as Integrity Plus Metal. It also includes the one-time cost for producing a new die of $12,250 by outside sources.

Does checking sentence length allow you to catch all the glitches in your sentences? No, it doesn't. But it does let you get a maximum return of improvement from a minimum of time and effort, because it allows you to focus quickly on potential problems.

Frozen Action

The easiest way to sound like a bureaucrat is to use words that indicate frozen action. On the contrary, you want to express action in verb forms, to heighten the sense of doing. This sense of doing is essential in recommendations.

Scenario

You know that, unless targeted at specific problems, revision can continue forever. But something still bothers you about the revised version of your executive summary on data collection (in Decision 13). Reading over the final sentence, you decide it seems chewy, hard to swallow, even though you've cut it up into bite-sized chunks with numerals. Here it is:

☐ In those dropout-prevention programs where the cooperative approach can be viable, we have identified six conditions that can increase data comparability: 1) national leadership in directing the development of model criteria and standardized forms, by either a federal agency or a national association; 2) states' recognition of the need for dropout-prevention data; 3) federal funding to support data collection activities; 4) designated national-level staff to work with state officials; 5) state officials' involvement in the design of the systems; and 6) federal statutes to encourage cooperation in data collection.

The six points in this sentence come off like the walking dead. Not one of the recommendations actually says to *do* something. They're static, even though they're intended to read as a call to action. In fact, in many of the points, the action being called for seems paralyzed in noun forms: "leadership," "recognition," "support," "involvement," and "cooperation." These words are frozen actions (sometimes called **nominalizations**), actions expressed as nouns.

Focus on Verb Forms

You rewrite the six points to wake up the action, focusing on verb forms to carry the message (and incidentally put them in more readable, or "See It," form):

In those dropout-prevention programs where we can use the cooperative approach, we recommend six steps to increase our ability to compare data:

1. a federal agency or a national association needs to lead the way in developing model criteria and standardized forms;
2. states need to recognize the necessity to collect data on dropout-prevention programs;
3. the federal government needs to support the states in collecting data;
4. the federal government needs to designate national-level staff to work with state officials;
5. state officials need to help design the systems; and
6. the Congress needs to write federal statutes that encourage the states to collect data.

Buried Sentence Core

A sentence is a marriage between a subject and a verb: for example, "The project succeeded." These are the **core** elements in any sentence, sometimes completed by an object: for example, "The project identified problems." Because the core carries the essential message in a sentence, the subject and verb are the high-impact words.

In adult communication, of course, you usually say more than a core statement. You usually add **modification**, in the form of single words, phrases, or clauses that further qualify the core statement. For instance, you could extend the core statement, above, in this way:

☐ The **review** project identified problems **with the program that occurred through misplaced priorities.**

These two elements, the core and the modification, are what the writer has to work with in reframing a sentence.

You know that the standard sentence length for most report writing is 17 to 25 words. If your core consists of three or four words, what's happening with the rest of the sentence? The answer is that adult communication relies on modifiers to show relationships and to enrich the meaning. Unfortunately, if you aren't careful, modification can also obscure the essential meaning carried by the core of the sentence.

Scenario

Let's say that, in the course of skimming through a report you are revising, you notice an unusually long sentence. Smelling trouble, you stop and actually count the words: 43. Here is the sentence.

☐ For its vehicles, DEA ordered dual-band radios which contain both VHF and UHF components to allow DEA agents in resident offices to access the FBI's VHF system, and switch to the UHF frequency band when entering the Boston or New York areas. (43 words)

You want to rewrite the sentence, but how do you sort out the basic pieces? You need a sort of verbal machete to hack through to the heart of a sentence that long.

Going to Pieces

The important question (your verbal machete) is **"Who is doing what?"**

In this sentence: **DEA ordered radios.** These words are the core or the heart of the sentence. Everything else in this sentence expands that basic information. So you can start with this smaller sentence:

☐ **For its vehicles, DEA ordered dual-band radios.**

What's left?

☐ which contain both VHF and UHF components to allow DEA agents in resident offices to access the FBI's VHF system, and switch to the UHF frequency band when entering the Boston or New York areas.

With this remaining part of the sentence, ask the same question: **Who (or what) is doing what?**
"(Something) contains VHF and UHF components." What is the something? "Dual-band radios." So, the revised sentence reads this way:

☐ **These dual-band radios contain both VHF and UHF components.**

What's left?

☐ to allow DEA agents in resident offices to access the FBI's VHF system, and switch to the UHF frequency band when entering the Boston or New York areas.

Ask the same question as before: **Who (or what) is doing what?**
"(Something) allows DEA agents." What is the something? In this case, the radios. So your sentence now says:

☐ **The radios allow DEA agents in resident offices to access the FBI's VHF system.**

Is there anything else the agents are allowed to do?

☐ **They are allowed to switch to the UHF frequency band when entering the Boston or New York areas.**

But this sentence is really a part of the previous sentence, so it should say:

☐ **The radios also allow DEA agents in resident offices to** switch to the UHF frequency band when entering the Boston or New York areas.

Putting the Pieces Together

Now, put all the pieces together. The rewrite reads like this:

☐ For its vehicles, DEA ordered dual-band radios. These dual-band radios contain both VHF and UHF components. The radios allow DEA agents in resident offices to access the FBI's VHF system. They also allow DEA agents in resident offices to switch to the UHF frequency band when entering the Boston or New York areas.

Testing the Rewrite

Count the words to see if sentence length is better.

☐ For its vehicles, DEA ordered dual-band radios. (8 words) These dual-band radios contain both VHF and UHF components. (10 words) The radios allow DEA agents in resident offices to access the FBI's VHF system. (14 words) They also allow DEA agents in resident offices to switch to the UHF frequency band when entering the Boston or New York areas. (23 words)

You seem to have made an improvement. But shorter sentences are not always better. When you rewrite, you need to make sure that your sentences still "sound" okay. Read this passage aloud. Notice that it "sounds" choppy?

The source of the choppiness seems to be the first two short sentences. Can you combine them? For example:

☐ **For its vehicles, DEA ordered dual-band radios that contain both VHF and UHF components.** (15 words)

When you combine this sentence with the entire passage, the revision reads this way:

☐ **For its vehicles, DEA ordered dual-band radios that contain both VHF and UHF components.** (15 words) **The radios allow DEA agents in resident offices to access the FBI's VHF system.** (14 words) **They also allow**

DEA agents in resident offices to switch to the UHF frequency band when entering the Boston or New York areas. (23 words)

Our final word count per sentence is 15, 14, and 23. All sentences are under the suggested 30 words and much easier to understand than the original 43 words.

Why the shorter sentences are easier to understand is not just a matter of length. As we have shown with the sentence core, the way a sentence is put together has a lot to do with readability. And one more factor comes into play: your building materials.

Bricks and Mortar

You can say that the words you build sentences with are like bricks and mortar. That is, some key words are like the bricks of meaning, distinct to your thought (e.g., vehicle, agency, access, radio, frequency). These bricks in your thought structure need to be held together by mortar words, the generally small, frequently used words that appear over and over in your sentences (e.g., for, its, that, both, and, in, the). Generally, the more bricks you have in proportion to mortar, the more meaning the reader has to deal with. When you pack too much into a sentence, you are likely to increase the proportion of bricks to mortar. The problem, then, is not just sentence length, but sentence density. The meaning crumbles under its own weight.

Decision 14 Worksheet

Use a sample of your own professional writing.

1. Skim down the margin looking for the extra white spaces that mark the ends of sentences.
2. Mark any place that has very long (about three lines) or very short (about half a line) sentences.
3. Check that the content of the short sentences is appropriate to receive the emphasis the short sentence naturally provides.
4. Count the words in the long sentences and check where they fall on the Readability chart above.
5. Graph the lengths, if you wish.
6. Decide whether you need to shorten or lengthen sentences.
7. Examine all actions to determine where your sentence core should be.
8. Look for possible frozen action, words ending in "ion," "ness," "ity," or "ance."

A REVISER'S BILL OF RIGHTS

1. You have the right to separate your "self" from your product.
2. You have the right to consider your first draft tentative.
3. You have the right to know whether the original writing situation still holds.
4. You have the right to use revising to clarify your own thinking.
5. You have the right to set priorities on the revisions you'll make.
6. You have the right to revise for the theme or message before you revise the sentences.
7. You have the right to specify the type of feedback you want from your reviewer.
8. You have the right to consider your reviewer's preferences.
9. You have the right to accept or reject review comments—after giving them serious consideration.
10. You have the right to let proofreading be your last priority.

CHAPTER SIX

The Review Process

Surviving Review

Perhaps you respond to the prospect of being reviewed about the same way you respond to going to the dentist—you may know it's good for you, but it hurts, and why does it cost so much? It's an interesting question to pose and ponder: if you could do without review, would you?

Review offers you certain advantages as a writer: it gives you a chance to get feedback and it allows you to share final responsibility for clarity of the text. Review also allows upper management to add information that may not be available to you. Moreover, it offers an opportunity for building consensus within the organization, a process which, without documents to review, might be even more elusive than it is. For these reasons, review usually makes your document better.

Review Problems

But let's not mince words: review has its problems. It can lengthen the timeframe for producing your document, sometimes causing you to miss milestones or deadlines. And even with a word processor, it can be a pain to incorporate changes. It takes time—no matter how fast your computer. In addition, tactless review comments can bruise the self-esteem of a conscientious writer.

In the review process, the most common source of frustration may occur between you and your immediate supervisor. You may feel as if you're playing ping-pong. Every draft you write comes right back with a request for more changes. You can wind up feeling lost in the review comments. Four hundred comments is common for a thirty-page draft, but horror stories of 1800 comments on a single draft are true, if not common. The real problem with this number of review comments occurs when the reviewer gives no sense of which comments are more important and which comments are less so. Reviewers who make comments without regard to priorities fail to give the writer a game plan—an idea about what's most important in the reviewer's mind, or what to address first. In that situation, where do you begin?

A writer can unwittingly increase the extent of review by sending drafts forward prematurely. Here's a scenario that involves a writer in a large organization. As a team leader, he has to compose a report that will go up to the project manager for approval. He and his team have done many things right to prepare for the report, including meeting with management to determine an outline. Everyone considers the meeting to have been hugely successful, with many good suggestions made that the team leader tries to follow when he composes the draft. The following is the calendar of his review process.

Day 1. After three weeks of work, he finishes drafting chapters 1 and 2. He gives the drafts to his immediate supervisor, while continuing to work on chapter 3.

Day 7. He gets chapter 1 back, but not 2. He goes back to work on chapter 1, and resubmits it a day later (draft 2 of chapter 1).

Day 9. He gets chapter 2 back, and chapter 1 again, with more changes. He incorporates the changes and resubmits both chapters (draft 3 of chapter 1 and draft 2 of chapter 2). The same day, he gets chapter 1 returned with more changes, which he immediately incorporates and resubmits (draft 4 of chapter 1).

Day 12. Chapters 1 and 2 come back with changes. At this point, he gets smart. He sits on chapters 1 and 2 until he's finished chapter 3. (Spending so much time on 1 and 2 isn't allowing him to work on chapter 3.)

Day 19. He submits all three chapters to his immediate supervisor once more for review. He's completed five drafts of chapter 1, three of chapter 2, and one of 3. Four has not been written yet.

It's now six weeks since the team leader started drafting—and the project manager has yet to see a word. In fact, in the eyes of his organization, he hasn't "officially" started the review process at all.

This writer has been involved in a means of review called document cycling, in which a draft passes back and forth between a writer and an immediate supervisor—typically three times. The goal of this cycling is to create consensus at the level of your work unit. In an organization with a flattened hierarchy, such as many scientific research organizations, this level of cycling may be enough. In a highly hierarchical organization, however, with many levels of review, this cycling may occur a number of times between units, each time with the object of building consensus within the levels of the organization. Since the document is likely to cycle back across the original writer's desk with each new level of review, the writer may actually wind up incorporating as many as twenty different sets of review comments.

A writer faced with the task of incorporating all these changes may well question the worth of the review process. In fact, the writer in this scenario hasn't acted to get the most out of the review process. All he will get, in fact, is confused—by an endless succession of review comments. By submitting the draft in fragments, he has effectively ensured that the review will take place in fragments.

The writer needs to focus his requests for review in one of two ways. He can either wait to send all five chapters at one time, or send chapter 1 through the process until it meets his supervisor's approval. Often a first chapter contains important indications of the writing situation. It can be worthwhile to iron these issues out before drafting substantial additional material.

The Pluses of Review

Given these difficulties, you may find it hard to accept that review makes the product better. To get the most out of review, the writer has to realize that this process of moving the document up through the hierarchy is the organization's way of achieving ownership of the document during the writing process.

If you don't learn how to handle the cycling, you can be overwhelmed by review changes. While not everything is under your control, you need to anticipate and plan for review changes as much as possible. The review process will be challenge enough without your adding to your own burden.

Through review, the organization attempts to make sure the document includes all the information necessary, and that it suits the context for which it is intended. To that extent, the review process takes the report back to the writing situation and cycles through it again, possibly in a way that takes into account information the writer couldn't have had access to. (For instance, you're trying to write a proposal that includes TRW as a subcontractor; what you don't know, and what it's illegal for anyone in the hierarchy to tell you, is that TRW is trying to acquire your company.) The review process turns a draft into a document, the organization into its author.

You might think of it this way: when you use the Decision Method to plan, and get management to sign off on your planning, you are engaging in a form of quality assurance for your document. Similarly, the review process is the organization's way of conducting quality control on the document before it, so to speak, goes to the customer—the intended reader.

You can survive review with your ego and your reputation intact if you follow some guidelines.

Before Review

Share planning documents. Make sure that when you submit the draft, you aren't handing your manager any surprises. Submit at least your statement of purpose and statement outline for approval before you draft.

Focus the review. Ask for attention to problems that you feel require feedback. And make sure you time the submission of your document in such a way that the reviewer can avoid overwhelming you or being overwhelmed. Don't submit the draft in fragments, and try to allow sufficient time for a thoughtful review before deadline.

Get your manager to buy into the document as early as possible. Your early decisions about the writing situation and structure will produce working papers, such as analysis of the readers or statements of the problems or outlines. If you're writing as a member of a group, then your manager may well be participating already. If you're writing as an individual, show your planning documents to your manager before you start to draft. Your manager can raise objections, make suggestions, shift a focus—before you have invested time and energy in drafting the document.

Use the editor. If your office has an editor, ask for some feedback or talk through some of the issues bothering you about the draft. Many editors can offer a clear view of what the issue is and how to approach it. Once defined, you may find changes easy to make.

Use your mentor. If this document is important, run a draft by your mentor (not necessarily the same person as your manager). Why? Increasingly, research suggests that one of the most significant changes reviewers make is to adjust a text to their sense of the organization's constraints. People higher in the organization are sometimes higher because they have a good "organizational sense." Your mentor can help you learn the organization as he or she makes suggestions for revisions.

Use peer review. Before taking a draft to your manager or mentor, run it by a peer. Peers (and not just the resident editor) can offer helpful reactions. You can ask for a general reaction, but you'll get better (and faster) results if you focus your peer on *one* particular area or issue. You might want him or her to look at the tone of one section or to read for missing steps. Peer review can help you put a better foot forward. (One word of caution: sharks are real; choose your peer carefully. If this person puts down other people, he or she will probably put you down too. Choose someone else.)

Schedule a meeting. Review is an oral process as well as a written one. Make sure you meet with your manager to go over his or her written comments. You may be able to clear up a question your manager had, or offer a perspective he or she hadn't considered. And hearing your manager describe his or her changes will help you understand your manager's priorities for revision.

During Review

Don't take it personally. Most reviewers seem focused on trying to get the "best possible" text out the door. Their review comments may lack tact and grace, but they are rarely intended as a personal assault on the writer. Focus on the substance of what they say. They may actually want to help you improve.

Don't sweat the small stuff. Different people reading a draft will respond to different nuances in the content and the style. If a suggestion doesn't change your meaning, do it—unless you have an immediate time constraint or unless you will need to go through the entire review process again. This suggestion is really a variation on "choose your battles." Something will probably arise that you feel strongly about; that's when you want the discussion and the disagreements. Otherwise, take the suggestion.

After Review

Learn from the comments. Many reviewers may know more about the organization and the culture or may know it differently from you—no matter what your level within the organization. Let them teach you what works and what doesn't from their perspective. Try to understand the reasoning behind their comments. Some people mistakenly think that using the revised text as boilerplate for another product will do the trick. Instead, you want to *understand* the thinking behind the review changes, so that you can apply it to your next product. Now, some veteran writers may have a hard time explaining reasons to you; they just know them. Trust their sense, but try to articulate the principle for yourself.

Relax. Review may seem excruciating as you go through it, but it will end. Focus on getting the job done. Some adrenaline is a good idea, but don't turn yourself inside out.

One Last Note

Change is inevitable. Like everything else in life, organizations are dynamic and sometimes seemingly fickle. Although you may have invested a great deal of time in a project, the organization may shift priorities or may set up new procedures. One Washington organization encouraged using letters as a way of reporting to clients quickly. Just about the time everyone embraced the new format, the head of the organization decided that too many letter reports were going out and that they needed to emphasize the traditional report again. No amount of planning could have anticipated this shift.

The lesson here is that you can't control everything. But the Decision Method can help you feel more in control of the writing process, because it helps you to work with—not in spite of—other people. And, in an organization, other people are the essence of the writing process.

Conducting Review

If you supervise others, you might dread conducting a review almost as much as you dread being reviewed yourself. You might feel that you never get what you ask for in a draft, and it's hard to figure out what to say or do to make the draft better. And maybe you hate to be the heavy, the one with the bad news in the form of review comments. You might find yourself, day after day, putting the draft you have to review at the bottom of your In basket.

Yet at its best, reviewing documents may be productive in numerous ways. Ideally, document review should have three goals. The first goal is strategic: review should establish the appropriateness of the document to the organization's goals and culture. The second goal is technical: review should improve the accuracy of the draft, whether of the facts, or of the punctuation, grammar, and spelling. These are short-term goals, focused on improving the document itself. The third goal is a long-range goal: staff development. Ideally, review will improve not only the document, but also the skills of your staff. In so doing, your review efforts will serve the short-term goals of future reviews, for you will have increased your staff's ability to write appropriately and accurately.

You can achieve these goals by following some guidelines for reviewing a draft.

Before Review

Collaborate with your staff. You can avoid surprises at the review stage if you monitor and guide projects from the start. Do this by asking for interim products that keep you in touch with your staff's planning strategies. Make sure you see at least a statement of purpose and a full statement outline before the writer drafts.

Ask the writer what to review for. To focus your own reading, always inquire about matters of interest to the writer in the draft, or potential problem areas. This information will not only help you focus your review efforts, it will also tell you how receptive and self-aware the writer is.

Check the planning documents before you review. As with any management task, decide on your objectives: what are you trying to accomplish by reviewing this document? Use the planning documents to remind yourself of project dimensions you have negotiated with your staff.

While You Review

First tie your hands. Read the document without a pencil in hand the first time through.

Use structured reading. You want to see whether you can discern the overall message from the advance organizers. If you can't, you need to direct your review comments to solving the major problems of structure before your review goes any further. The document will have to go back to the writer for restructuring, and all of the sentences will change. The sentences in which you're inclined to change punctuation and wording are likely to change anyway in the second draft, as the writer puts the whole thing together differently. Use the checklist for structured reading, perhaps even returning the checklist to the writer.

Discipline yourself to follow this method even if you're a details manager, even if you're an inductive thinker who likes to work on the fine points first to get yourself in gear. Don't waste review efforts, and don't overload the writer with superfluous changes.

Use tools to make your points more visible. To help make your comments a teaching aid, try to present them for easy visible comprehension. For instance, use Post-it ™ notes to flag important points. Or use several colors of highlighter to mark different kinds of problem. The extra effort you use in presentation will pay off in higher comprehension of your points by the writer.

Distinguish matters of substance from matters of personal taste. This point means simply this: don't change it if it doesn't

STRUCTURED READING FOR REVIEWERS

Advance Organizers

Is an executive summary provided?

Does the title indicate the major theme of the report? Do the headings and subheadings mark major sections of the report?

Are summary statements used as overviews to forecast information for my reader?

Do the topic sentences tell the story of the document?

Does the typographic arrangement emphasize the main points? Are highlighting techniques used to emphasize main points? Are typographic arrangement or highlighting techniques overused?

Do graphics emphasize important points?

Paragraphs

Do clusters of paragraphs or sections provide a unified context? Is the order logical?

Do individual paragraphs support the topic sentence?

Do guide words or transitions help the reader predict the points of the document?

Sentences

Are any sentences too long or too short?

Do sentences place important information in the sentence core?

Are sentences concise and precise?

Words and Phrases

Are words and phrases used grammatically and idiomatically?

Is jargon a problem in the document?

Are there spelling or punctuation errors?

have to be changed. Not everything has to be written in your personal style to be effective. Writers will recognize and resent having to sound too much like you, and your teaching efforts in other areas will have less credibility as a consequence.

Relate your suggestions to the goals of the product. This point is a corollary of the previous one: writers will respect your suggestions when they feel the suggestions are directed to your common goal of fulfilling the assignment.

Remember your own blind spots. That is, don't overplay your strengths. Remember to deal with those areas that you know in your own writing you tend not to value—and respect writing strengths that you may not share. You will find, incidentally, that in this regard you will learn by teaching.

After Review

Set up a meeting. Try to avoid conveying review comments through one medium only—always try to combine written comments with oral feedback. Face-to-face communication allows you to detect misperceptions and correct misunderstandings—on your own or the writer's part. Additionally, it allows you to set up and reinforce your priorities in revision of the document, or reconsider them with the writer's help.

Listen. Seek feedback about the draft from the writer. Managers and staff tend to have expertise in different areas. You, as manager, probably have greater understanding of the situation in which the document is to be used. You can solve many review problems by finding out the writer's perception of the writing situation, since many drafting errors occur out of misconceptions about the writing situation. You have an opportunity in that case to orient the writer more fully to the organization you both represent. Similarly, the writer is probably in more immediate command of the pertinent facts than you are. Try to remember that he or she made certain writing choices because the choices made sense in the light of the facts. Listening might help you reconcile your perceptions with those of the writer.

Set priorities. Make sure you specify to the writer which changes are most important to make. Writers can be overwhelmed by review comments and can feel paralyzed and unable to revise.

Especially in a deadline situation, your efforts to establish priorities will ensure that the "must fixes" are attended to. These might include changes in those areas that most affect credibility: executive summary, headings, topic sentences, spelling, and punctuation.

Set up a win/win situation. Use review to improve, not judge. This point holds true both for product and person—decide whether you want to play coach or gatekeeper in your role as reviewer. Sometimes you will need to be in the role of gatekeeper, not letting a document get out until it meets organizational standards.

But more often, you should try to be the coach, viewing your comments as suggestions rather than requirements as much as possible. Your goal, in this case, is to make a long-term contribution to the organization by developing another good writer.

When Things Are Bad

You, as a manager, may have a staff member who as a writer really is below average. How do you deal with that situation? Telling the person that his or her writing is poor, unintelligible, or lousy is likely to cause morale problems as well as encourage the person to become defensive. Generally you can follow the KEY and PROBE process to analyze the situation. This process identifies five KEY questions to move you from identifying the problem to reaching a solution, and it uses PROBE questions to move you toward specificity.

You can use this method with any writer, but it is particularly helpful in difficult and sensitive situations. And bear in mind that, as a manager, you probably can't solve serious writing problems without help. Many organizations have extensive internal training courses as well as access to outside sources. In addition, a number of excellent grammar and punctuation review packages are available in software. Any or all of these resources may help, and you want to use them to address the problem. If you can, avoid passing it on to the next manager.

In Sum

Review is inevitable; like death and taxes, it won't go away. So, perhaps the best way to think about this whole topic is to remember the advice above and this last point:

> The strongest drive
>
> is not love or hate.
>
> It is one person's need
>
> to ~~change~~ another's copy.

modify / alter ~~advise~~ / rewrite ~~amend~~ / change / ~~chop to pieces~~

Manager's Checklist For Writing Problems

What is the general writing problem?

- ☐ Does the message lack clear analysis?
- ☐ Does the presentation lack clear structure?
- ☐ Is the language inappropriate?
- ☐ Is the English incorrect?

What is the specific writing problem?

- ☐ Does the document fail to fulfill its purpose?
- ☐ Are the reader's needs not generally met?
- ☐ Is the subject treated too narrowly or broadly?
- ☐ Is the writer's stance inappropriate?
- ☐ Are the facts inaccurate?
- ☐ Is the data irrelevant?
- ☐ Are the theoretical assumptions invalid?
- ☐ Is the reasoning inappropriate to the purpose of the document?
- ☐ Is the document organized without a clear, apparent structure?
- ☐ Has the writer failed to use headings to increase the accessibility of the message?
- ☐ Has the writer failed to use topic sentences to open paragraphs?
- ☐ Has the writer failed to arrange points in a logical progression?
- ☐ Are the sentences too long or too short?
- ☐ Are the sentences illogical?
- ☐ Does the writer use inappropriate terms?
- ☐ Does the writer use jargon?
- ☐ Is the grammar incorrect?
- ☐ Are spelling and punctuation incorrect?
- ☐ Is the language not idiomatic?

How much does the problem matter?

- ☐ Can I solve it by simple editing?
- ☐ Does solving the problem require redrafting the document?
- ☐ Does solving the problem require that I redraft the document myself?

What is the source of the problem?

- ☐ Does the writer lack skill in English?
- ☐ Does the writer lack composition skills?
- ☐ Does the writer lack sufficient technical expertise for the topic of the report?
- ☐ Does the writer lack experience in this type of document?
- ☐ Did I fail to give the writer enough information about the assignment?
- ☐ Is the assignment complex?

What will solve the writer's problem?

- ☐ Training in English as a Second Language?
- ☐ Review of the basics of English grammar?
- ☐ Training in written communication?
- ☐ Further research or education?
- ☐ Giving the writer models of this type of document?
- ☐ Explaining my expectations in greater detail?
- ☐ Monitoring the progress of the assignment to help shape the thought process?

CHAPTER SEVEN

The Dynamics of Writing in an Organization

Collaborating in Organizations

For writers in large organizations, pride of ownership goeth before a fall. In an organization, very often the unacknowledged author of any document is the organization itself. Since organizations are made up of people, the act of authoring necessarily becomes an act of collaboration. Several people may share responsibility for drafting, and numerous reviewers may change the draft. Pride of ownership must give way to pride of contribution.

When it works well, collaboration can mean synergy. It is a process in which 1 + 1 = 3, in which the whole is greater than the sum of the parts. Your own collaborative products can be better than any single person can make them. (Remember, the U.S. Constitution is a collaborative effort.)

But group writing has a bad reputation. To say that a document "reads like something written by a committee" is no compliment. And nearly any person on the job for more than a year has a horror story to tell about a group project. How can you avoid the pitfalls? What can you do to get the most out of collaboration?

What to Do About Other People

Every person brings different strengths and weaknesses to the writing process, and an ideal group interaction will draw on every member's strengths, while compensating for each member's individual weaknesses. Your group can work most successfully if you follow some basic ground rules.

No individual is the author. In group projects, no one person should emerge as the primary author. No matter who coordinates the project, the group is the author of the product. And quite often, as in a proposal, the organization, not any single group, is the author. Individuals have to learn to let go of control over the project, and identify with the group.

Nobody's good at everything. While every group needs a leader, no one person should always be in control. As different skills are required for different aspects of the writing process, leadership should and will shift. One person might be a far-seeing strategist in analyzing the writing situation, but hits the wall with outlining. Another person will take leadership for outlining in order to move the project forward. Groups that actively look for the leadership to change tend to produce better documents.

Everybody's good at something. This reminder is the other side of the "Nobody's good at everything" coin. It can help you tolerate a seeming lack of contribution from another member of the group (or from yourself) early in the process. Someone who has trouble conceptualizing about the writing situation, for instance, might turn out to be the detail person— the one with command of the facts when it comes time to organize your materials. Even if you find the earlier decisions more difficult, attend to these decisions and look forward with confidence to your later contribution.

All ideas are worth a hearing. Whether you're making writing decisions or your product is being reviewed within the organization, give each idea a hearing. In the writing process, you need to begin by brainstorming answers and solutions to problems. The more contributions your group generates, the larger the pool of possibilities will be. The larger your pool of possibilities, the better your basis for choosing. The same principle holds for review. Reviewers offer you other possibilities for phrasing and sometimes for interpretation.

In considering others' ideas, follow a two-step process: first, accept the contribution as a possibility, then sort and select. You may find in the brainstorming phase, for instance, that seemingly pointless or silly suggestions will give you an idea for narrowing down the possibilities. Similarly, a review comment that seems to come from left field can provide the clue to organizing the report more effectively.

Dissension is healthy at certain stages of the process. While most groups start out politely, establishing roles and rules for play, disagreements will arise—and maybe early in the game. Cherish these disagreements, for in a sense they are the signs of life: as ideas spark to life and catch fire they generate heat. Along with this heat, your group will be shedding light on the project at hand. Without conflict to resolve, most groups will fail to generate commitment to the ideas under discussion. Consequently, a group that proceeds without any conflict may fail to accomplish much.

Everyone is responsible. In a group, everyone needs to pull his or her own weight. Even if your strength comes to the fore later in the game, you still need to be a part of the group from the beginning. This means that you must monitor your own participation in the group, making sure you neither dominate all the time nor withdraw all the time.

You also need to monitor your interactions with others. Too often groups fail to progress with a project because they get caught in their stereotypes of individuals. They fail to count the contribution of one person because they perceive that person as a generalization based on sex, race, nationality, religion, dress, or hygiene. During the course of the project, you should take a periodic, but very conscious, reality check about the basis for your judgments of the contributions of others.

All parts of the process are necessary. One advantage of working in a group is that it's unlikely everyone will have the same weaknesses—and be tempted to skip the same parts of the process. Don't let one person's strengths and weaknesses dominate: don't fall into the same hole as, say, the leader and be tempted to skip the part the leader doesn't like. Only if you cycle fully through the Decision Cycle will you be able to take advantage of everyone's strengths and compensate for everyone's inevitable weaknesses.

What to Do About Yourself

In some respects, the Decision Method is an approach to dealing with writer's block. It suggests ways to get started, ways to avoid the blank page syndrome through step-by-step analysis of the decisions necessary for writing. But even following the Decision Method, you can encounter problems. Given human nature, you are likely to feel more comfortable with some parts of the Decision Cycle than with others.

In fact, most people will have a blind spot on the Decision Cycle. And that can be a problem. Think about your own response to the Decision Cycle—do you have a reservation or two about one element of it (situation, facts, concepts, structure)? You may well find that you tend to value one element less than the others, and you will tend to skimp on the decisions related to that element.

Here is a model of the Decision Cycle. Now that you've had an opportunity to work through the whole process, you might just take a moment to think about which element you felt most comfortable with, and which the least.

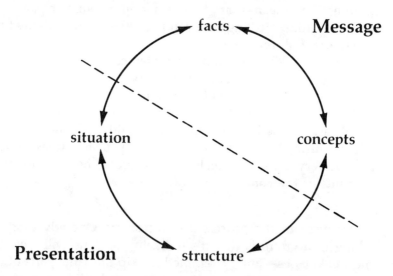

When you think about the way you use the Decision Cycle, you probably find that you are well aware of your strength, and that you tend to play to it. Why shouldn't you? Your strength allows you to do what you like to do, and do it well. Probably you have chosen a profession that suits your strength and reinforces that strength daily. It goes without saying that your strength will be your greatest asset in writing.

But writing well is a matter of learning to expose and deal with your weaknesses—and everybody has them. In fact, you might think of your least preferred element of the Decision Cycle as the flip side of the coin, with your strongest preference on the other side. Overplaying your strength, to the exclusion of developing your weakness, can lead to writer's block. Something will be missing in the process, and you may find yourself disinclined to search out the problem and solve it—because it involves something you don't like to do.

Recognizing Strengths and Blind Spots

How can you recognize your strengths and your blind spots? Besides your intuitive sense of what works and what doesn't, you can ask coworkers. They often have a clearer sense of the situation. You can also look for yourself in the following descriptions.

Situation. Situation is the people part of the Decision Cycle. It deals with the strategy of filling perceived needs, of finding out what the readers are like, and how you can best communicate with them. You have a strength here if you're adept at handling the politics of communication, if purpose is the first thing you think about when you write, if audience analysis is second nature to you, if you're always aware of the image you project when you write.

On the other hand, you have a blind spot here if you feel it's somehow "cheating" to consider the audience, unwholesome to strategize about purpose, demeaning to formulate your role as the writer, and insulting to think about what your readers already know or don't know. You may feel that these considerations jeopardize your objectivity, even your integrity as a writer. The danger, of course, is that your written product won't come across to your readers—that it won't do the job it needs to do in the situation in which it will be read.

Facts. If you are a facts person, you may have a good grasp of statistics, a feel for numbers. Detail probably interests you, and you probably enjoy collecting details and are good at pulling up details that others forget. (Did you know that Madame Tussaud made the death mask of Marat?) You may well have mastered complex techniques for collecting, recording, and compiling data in your mind and on paper. Few things bother you more than those people in a group who jump to conclusions and then can't prove their point with facts. Data bits are what you eat for breakfast.

A real "facts" person would be shocked at the idea of a blind spot here—what else is there (as Sergeant Friday would say) but the facts? How could anyone ignore the facts? In truth, if your blind spot is facts, you may not be ignoring them—you may simply jump from facts to concepts too quickly to retain the facts. Because you may value facts largely as a means of reaching conclusions, you may assimilate facts without keeping them separate and distinct. A facts blind spot often manifests itself as a failure to keep complete, accessible notes. As a result, you often have to refocus on facts—even maybe collect them a second time—so that you have the "proof" to allow a reader to reach the same conclusions you have. Your writing may be characterized by airy leaps of logic or unsupported generalizations.

Concepts. If your strength is concepts, you probably think of yourself as an ideas person. You will tend to see more than one way to say or do something, sometimes to your detriment. You may see connections almost automatically, and you may be good at synthesizing. Interpretation means more to you than the facts themselves. You tend to value "big picture" thinking, and determining the overview is rarely a problem for you. In a group, your nemesis is the individual who continually challenges, "How can you say that?" when your response is, "How can you not?"

If you skimp on concepts, you may be a person with an extraordinary respect for facts—the notion that "the facts speak for themselves" is one that you value. You may feel so strong a respect for facts that you may tend to feel that they carry the meaning—a meaning of which, in your own head, you may be well aware. But you may fall down in interpreting facts for others, in establishing clear relationships, in drawing the big picture for the reader. In fact, you may be suspicious of "big picture" thinking, as if it represented a neglect of the real world, a failure to keep one's feet on the ground. While your writing may be full of facts, you run the danger of making your writing a data dump, with insufficient differentiation or context.

Structure. If structure is your strength, you probably have a reputation for logic. You probably find it fairly easy to establish priorities in your communication. Hierarchies of thought come naturally to you. You are good at putting the puzzle pieces in their places. In fact, you may wonder what all the fuss is about outlining; you probably use outlines as a matter of course.

If you skimp on structure, you may do so because you tend to see it as dry—bare bones that lack the human touch, cold logic that doesn't speak of the subtleties of thought. You may distrust outlines, feeling limited, even constricted by them, as if an outline could interfere with your spontaneity of thought and responsiveness to your reader's needs. When you do use an outline, you may tend to leave information out. You may rely on nuances of tone, rather than consistency of structure, to carry your message to the reader. Consequently, while your writing may be full of pithy sentences, key statements may be hard for the reader to find.

What to Do about Blind Spots

Now that you've analyzed your blind spot, you'll probably want to work harder in that area. But how? Two solutions suggest themselves: team up with someone good at that element, and make use of throw-away documents.

Situation Solutions. One solution for situation blind spots is talking the project over with others. Collecting information about a project involves more than collecting technical data: it also involves finding out about the situation in which the product will be used. Ask yourself questions about the potential audience that show your readers in relation to yourself: "How are they similar to me?" and (perhaps more to the point) "How am I similar to them?"

You're probably aware of the advantages of having a mentor somewhere higher than you in the organization. If situation is your blind spot, a mentor might be the person to help you a great deal in this area. As someone who has had to learn the organization, he or she has necessarily had to learn to deal with the issue of writing situation. Since your mentor is by definition not your own boss, you may find that you can talk freely about a project without the fear of saying something "wrong."

Finally, be rigorous. Some people may be able to get away with merely talking themselves through analysis of the writing situation—but not you. Even if for your eyes only, write out the worksheets for Decisions 1 through 4. Only by exercising your hand can you be sure to exercise your mind in an area that doesn't appeal to you.

Facts Solutions. If facts are your blind spot, one simple, even mechanical solution is to use Post-it ™ notes to marshal the facts. This solution won't necessarily cure your blind spot ills if taking notes in the first place is your problem. But knowing that you have a technique for handling facts conceptually may make you more willing to collect them, and the Post-it ™ notes lend themselves easily to establishing patterns. In fact, for this blind spot, use mechanical solutions wherever possible. Besides Post-it ™ notes, use highlighters or colored pencils to code your notes. Use spreadsheet programs to help you keep the facts under control. Use file folders.

Concepts Solutions. If this is your blind spot, you want to use methods that allow you to build a conceptual framework out of the facts as you know them. Rely on storyboarding, since it allows you to see the patterns building out of the individual Post-it ™ notes. Be sure to work first on simply grouping the facts, then work up to drawing inferences from the groupings.

You might also try a technique called "freewriting." Without looking at your notes, simply write for ten minutes at a time—without stopping. Say whatever you want to say about the project, including simply reviewing your facts if you wish. Don't stop writing; if you run out of things to say, write out "Mary had a little lamb," or some other nonsense, just to keep your hand moving. (Remember that this is a throw-away document. The idea here is to sneak up on your thought process from behind.)

At the end of ten minutes, stop writing and read what you've written. Look for statements that represent interpretation or analysis, rather than simple repetition of the facts. Underline or highlight any such statements. Freewrite again and again until you have gathered a number of usable ideas. Collect the ideas by writing them out on individual 3 x 5 Post-it ™ notes or on a sheet of paper. (You may be able to use these statements to start an outline, by the way.)

Another technique is to pause periodically and say to yourself, "What I really mean is . . . ." This phrase can act as a trigger, forcing your mind to integrate facts into the message that you really want to send.

Structure Solutions. You aren't going to like the answer to this one. If structure is your weak point, you have to be rigorous about outlining. But you can make outlining easier, even relatively painless. Never try to begin a project with outlining (that goes without saying, now that you've assimilated the Decision Method). Instead, always work from the writing situation in developing an outline. Refer to the reader's anticipated questions about the subject in Decision 3. Once you have gathered your facts and analyzed your information, try to answer each of these questions in one sentence. Write each sentence on a 3 x 5 Post-it ™ note, and arrange the notes in order. Keep the process as flexible as possible, using Post-it ™ notes, so that you avoid feeling locked into the outline structure.

You can also try posting your notes on a wall. For many people, the shift to the vertical plane helps them *see* a structure more easily. Indeed, you want to be arranging the Post-it ™ notes so that they look like an outline—indenting some more than others. The movement to the vertical and the indenting seem to enhance your being able to visualize hierarchies in the thought structure, as you see the actual pattern of notes, some higher, some lower, on the wall before you.

Other Solutions

The solutions offered above can get you started, but they merely scratch the surface of the various blind spots. Your best solution is to become actively involved in solving the problems. Talk about writing with other people, and listen to what they have to say. Not every solution will work for you, of course, and it's important not to expect it to. (But it can be fun to listen to other people's pet methods, and deduce where their strengths and blind spots must be.) Be flexible, but don't put yourself in completely unfamiliar situations either. Instead, try out one new method each time you start a writing project. Eventually, you can develop a repertoire of ways that work for you.

CHAPTER EIGHT

Computers Can Help: A Note From the Publisher[1]

Ask most people whose jobs involve writing about how they use computers and they'll invariably start talking about how their word processors have changed their lives. They'll start by talking about how many drafts they can now crank out, and then they'll move on to how word processors have made spelling errors as extinct as yellow fever.

But computers can do a lot more. They can help you improve the organization of large documents, search standard reference books with a few keystrokes, develop an appropriate and consistent style, avoid making errors in grammar and usage, orchestrate the review of a draft by all the members of a committee, add graphics, talk to other writers, and so on.

In fact, for the IBM-PC alone, at least 50 products are being sold whose only purpose is to assist you with the writing process. In this chapter, you'll get a glimpse of those we think are today's brightest stars.

Sorry, you Macintosh fans, but all the programs described here were tested on IBM-PCs. However, a good number of them are available for you to use as well.

---

[1]This chapter courtesy of Steve Frankel, Publisher, PC Press and President, Scandinavian PC Systems.

Outlining Tools

So far, it's been much easier to develop an outline with a pencil and yellow pad than to do it with most word processors. The trouble has been that the mechanics of doing the indents and remembering whether to use an upper or lower case letter get in the way of your creative thought process.

But lately a few good outliners have come onto the market. They not only take care of the mechanics for you, but they also do neat tricks such as renumbering the entire outline in an instant if you delete or add something to it.

Two of the most sophisticated outliners are "free." They're the outlining tools contained within **Microsoft Word Version 5** (Microsoft) and **WordPerfect 5.0** (WordPerfect).

While both can do the job perfectly well (no pun intended) and can be mastered in less than 30 minutes, it's the **Microsoft Word 5.0** outliner that's the real star. It links your outline to the actual document you create, so that if you later decide to move a section of your outline forward or backward, the text linked to that section of the outline in the action document will also move. Thus the outliner becomes not only a valuable planning tool, but an even more valuable revision tool that can save you countless hours if you've got to completely reorganize a lengthy and complex report.

Further, even if you didn't create an outline in the first place, **Microsoft Word 5.0** lets you add the outline later, so that you can use it to facilitate making revisions.

However, you've got to realize that WordPerfect 5.0 is the best-selling word processor in the world and has become a *de facto* standard in many places. Also, their free "800" help-line support is the best you'll find anywhere.

If you don't use either of these powerhouse word processors, there's still an outliner you can use that's a real winner. It's called **InLine** (Compusense) and is inexpensive. It can also be mastered in less than 30 minutes. In fact, **InLine** is so easy to use that the manual is almost unnecessary. The program seems to anticipate your needs and do what you need it to do automatically. InLine's outlines can be exported to almost any word processor, so it's no trick at all to create an outline with **InLine** and then use that outline as a writing guide when you start writing with your word processor.

Reference Tools

One of the most useful programs designed to provide you with information at a keystroke is the **Key Notes AP Stylebook** (Digital Learning Systems). Once you load this into your computer, with a single keystroke you can leave your word processor and go right into an automated index of the entire 300-plus page stylebook developed by the Associated Press. It took us precisely 15 seconds to find out whether a semicolon should go inside or outside a quotation mark. Sure, we could have looked in the library for the hardcover version of the same book, but what if you're writing on an airplane on a portable PC?

Another slick program of this type is **Word Master** (Proximity). When it's loaded into your computer, you've got *Webster's Thesaurus* and the *Webster's Dictionary, Concise Edition,* on line. The thesaurus portion of this program is just like those contained in the more powerful word processors: it not only allows you to look for synonyms, but it also allows you to select a synonym and use a single keystroke to replace the word you originally used. The dictionary section of the program gives you the meanings, parts of speech, and inflection points for a word. The latter is especially useful when it comes to hyphenating a report, since the hyphenation routines included in most word processors are often inaccurate. The dictionary portion can also be used to give you the correct spelling of a particular word if you type in your best guess; unfortunately, unlike a spelling checker, it can't automatically search an entire document for misspelled words.

A program called **Choice Words** (Proximity) is very similar to **Word Master**. Proximity also sells **Word Finder**, which is the thesaurus portion of the program without the dictionary.

Still another program of this type is **TurboLightning** (Borland). It uses the Random House dictionary and thesaurus, and its claim to fame is an "autoproof" mode that beeps whenever you type in a word it doesn't recognize. It's like having your mother always peeking over your shoulder. Luckily, this mode can be turned off if this obtrusive tool turns you off. What you're left with is another superior and reliable reference tool.

Information Organizers

Among the hottest categories of software are the information organizers. These are programs that let you both make notes and retrieve them while you're using another program—whether it be your word processor or data base manager. The problem is that most programs in this category are just too complicated and take up too much memory in your computer.

However, there's one organizer you can use every day. It's called **Reference File** (Reference Software) and it's a quick and elegant way never to have to say "I forgot." This chapter was developed by running all of these programs (plus many others) and taking notes on their performance using **Reference File**. Then, when the chapter was actually written, those notes were available in seconds, already organized and alphabetized.

Another organizer that's well worth having is **Golden Retriever** (Wesware). It excels in finding phrases or references you may have written several years ago and that now reside in files that you've long forgotten. Just type in the words or phrases you want **Golden Retriever** to locate, and it will search your entire hard disk and list all the files containing those words. Further, it will show you the entire paragraph in which the phrase was found so that you can decide whether that's the file you want to see. Given that many people now have hard disks that contain more than 10,000 files, this program is worth its weight in gold if it can find you the files you need. You can understand why they gave the program its name.

Screen Grabbers

There's no room in this book to give you a full rundown on programs that create drawings and illustrations. That topic deserves its own book and indeed several on the topic are available. However, one program must be mentioned. Its name is **Hotshot Graphics** (SymSoft) and it allows you to copy any screen image generated by any computer program into a file, then edit that screen image in any conceivable way. Thus you can capture a screen image generated by your spreadsheet that shows financial projections for a project and erase the columns that aren't needed. You can give the image a headline written in large, bold type, shade the most important figures so that they stand out, and create little boxes with writing in them that can be used to point to and explain certain figures. This program is useful for anyone who creates sophisticated reports.

Grammar Checkers

The two leading grammar checkers are **Grammatik IV** (Reference Software) and **RightWRITER 3.1** (RightSoft). Both of these programs do a good job of screening your writing and highlighting what may be grammatical errors or poor usage.

If you haven't used programs like this for several years, give them a second try—they're now much more sophisticated. They're now true grammar parsers. This means that they actually take sentences apart, word-by-word, and determine which word is the subject, which is the verb, etc. Once this task is done, it's relatively easy for them to identify many kinds of common grammatical errors. They also look for phrases that have been included in their various dictionaries, which include everything from cliches to sexist language. When they find a match between something you've written and something in their dictionaries, they issue you a warning.

These programs also generate the most popular readability indices: the Flesch-Kincaid, the Flesch Reading Ease, and the FOG Index. These indices evaluate the difficulty of what you've written in terms of your average sentence length and the average number of syllables contained in the words you've used. Readability index scores are now required for certain kinds of documents that are being written for various agencies of the U.S. Government. They are also mandated by some state laws, such as those trying to ensure that insurance policies will be understandable to most readers.

A word of warning, however: a good readability score doesn't guarantee a document that's easy to understand. For instance, if you *either* change all long words to shorter ones *or* arbitrarily divide all complex sentences into simple ones, your readability score will probably be acceptable. However, what you've produced may be less interesting and even harder to understand than before. Maybe that's why some Internal Revenue Service (IRS) manuals have very good readability scores but are impossible for the average American to follow.

A very nice additional feature of **Grammatik IV** is that its developers are now making available special industry-specific dictionaries. These allow you to screen out of your writing those particular phrases which are considered cliches or objectionable in your particular field.

These programs are far from infallible and you'll probably choose to disregard a good share of their warnings. Neverthless, they're fine tools that allow you to do a preliminary edit of your own work so that you can remove the most obvious errors before someone else sees them. If such a program saves you embarrassment at work even once, it will be well worth the modest amount you paid for it.

Style Checkers

Of course, while grammar checkers deal with grammar and convention, style is another matter. No one writing style is the ideal style. Rather, you adopt a style appropriate for your intended audience and purpose. That's why when you write a love letter, you use a style very different from the one you use when you write a technical report. While grammar checkers can't help you decide what is an appropriate style, style checkers can.

Style checkers don't criticize your grammar or phrase selections. Rather, they look at the mechanical features which make a love letter different from a technical manual, then compare what you've written to models that have been programmed into them. As a result, they're able to identify those sentences that may be perfectly all right grammatically, but which aren't appropriate for the kind of writing you're trying to do.

For example, if you tell the program you're writing something aimed at young children, a style checker will help you ensure that your sentences are very short, that you've got relatively few long words in each sentence, that nearly all of the words you've used can be found on a list of the 450 most common words, and that the overall "readability" of the piece is below the sixth grade level as measured by popular readability indices such as the Flesch-Kincaid, the Flesch Reading Ease, and the FOG Index.

On the other hand, if you're writing an advertisement, the program will apply very different criteria when it looks at these variables. It will give you a lot of information related to other variables that determine the degree to which you're likely to keep adult readers' interest. For instance, the average number of short words you string together in a sentence affects the interest level. (Stringing lots of short words together was one of

Hemingway's tricks.) So does varying the length of sentences that adjoin each other.

Until the advent of the personal computer, you needed a good editor to get at these factors. An editor could, as the result of many years of experience, implicitly recognize these factors, make corrections, and gradually teach you to write in the styles that particular situations demand. However, now two programs exist that can help you do the same things automatically; that is, they can help you recognize whether what you've written is appropriate for the style you should be using.

The first of these programs is **Readability Plus** (Scandinavian PC Systems). It has nine styles programmed into it: general purpose writing, advertising copy, newspaper articles, novels, magazine articles, technical manuals, government writing, children's books, and bureaucratic gobbledegook (a style it teaches you to avoid). In seconds, it will read your file (it works with any word processor) and provide you with all the analyses described above, plus several others.

This program has received rave reviews from both the computer press and serious writers and has become the program-of-choice for people who must frequently vary their writing style (e.g., working on technical material in the morning and on advertising copy or press releases in the afternoon).

An even more powerful program is **Corporate Voice** (Scandinavian PC Systems). Here the analytic capabilities of **Readability Plus** have been combined with the analytic engine that Scandinavian PC Systems used to create the nine style models contained in that program. Thus, if you have **Corporate Voice**, you can use it to create custom models built around the best documents your firm has ever written. You can have the program analyze 20 winning proposals your division has written and develop a company proposal writing style against which future efforts can be evaluated. You can use this method to train junior staff to write in the style that has proven successful.

On the other hand, if you've been losing consistently, you can take winning documents written by your competitors and use **Corporate Voice** to analyze the stylistic differences between their writing and yours, and even create a style to emulate.

Similarly, with **Corporate Voice**, beginning writers can analyze Tom Clancy's military novels or Steven Spielberg's best.

scripts, and use the resulting style models as a point of departure for developing their own writing styles.

Another set of people who find **Corporate Voice** invaluable are those charged with reviewing the work of others. With the program they can—in seconds—contrast the work under review both with the best efforts the company has previously produced and with the so-called standard styles that come packaged with the program. This process can save hours of time and help reviewers pin-point problems they might otherwise have found difficult to articulate.

Groupware

Groupware is the name being given to software packages that are designed to allow a group of people to work on the same document. Several programs stand out in this category.

ForComment (Brøderbund) allows a writer to send diskettes containing a draft of a report to a group of reviewers, and then lets the reviewers make comments and suggest revisions. The program can then merge together the suggestions made by the different reviewers and generate a master review copy that the writer can evaluate. He can then make revisions, add his own comments, and make copies of this second version to distribute to the reviewers. This process can go on until consensus is reached, with the reviewers being able to see their own comments, those made by other reviewers, the writer's comments in response to the suggestions, and the changes that the writer has chosen to make.

Best of all, the reviewers cannot make changes in the master document—they can only suggest them. This feature is what makes the program far superior to merely distributing copies of your file to reviewers and letting them create their own version of the report—an invitation to chaos. **ForComment** is designed to invite collaboration, but leaves the writer in control.

If you do find yourself with several versions of the same file to deal with, then it's time to use our second pick in this category, **DocuLiner** (CompuLaw). It does what's called "redlining" in the legal profession: taking two versions of a document and highlighting the differences between them. With **DocuLiner**, you feed both versions into the program and you can get up to four different comparison reports. The composite draft is especially useful. It underlines text that was inserted in the newer draft, uses strikeout marks to highlight text that's been deleted, and puts text that's been moved in boldface type. At a glance you can see the extent of the mischief that's been worked on your masterpiece.

WordPerfect 5.0 can do almost the same thing. It can compare a version of a file on the screen with a version that was previously written and use redline and strikeout marks to highlight the changes. And **Microsoft Word Version 5** allows you to produce a redlined version of a document automatically as you revise it. However, it will not let you compare two documents that have previously been written, as the others can do.

Software Bridge (Systems Compatibility) and **Word for Word Professional** (Mastersoft) are in still another kind of groupware. These are document conversion programs that allow group members to use their own favorite word processors to create their portions of a document. Then the resulting formats can be combined into the one the principal author or corporation favors using. They're also useful for taking documents that were created several years ago on some of the early word processors such as **WordStar** and incorporating their contents into new documents created with **WordPerfect**, **Word**, **WordStar 2000**, etc.

Don't think you can avoid using one of these products by merely converting text created with different word processors into the universal ASCII text format. For, while nearly all modern word processors can do this conversion, it results in your losing all the formatting commands that were originally contained in those documents. The cost of reformatting even a single book-sized manuscript is much greater than the cost of one of these conversion programs, so not having one available is penny-wise and pound-foolish.

Desktop Publishers

Desktop publishers are programs that can take ordinary text and, with the help of a laser printer, make it appear as if it had been typeset. They can also do neat tricks such as snaking text around illustrations and incorporating a huge number of type styles and sizes on a particular page.

Again, this topic has several books written about it, but the general consensus today is that the front runners among desktop publishers are **Ventura Publisher (Xerox)** and **PageMaker (Aldus).** Once you learn to use them (it will take several months before you're really proficient), either of these programs can produce a complete newsletter, magazine, book or advertisement that looks as if a graphic designer and typesetter have spent weeks working on it.

Another word of warning: these are "use it or lose it" programs. Unless you plan to spend at least four hours a week using them, you're better off assigning someone else to learn them or hiring a consultant to use them for you. They require a commitment of time.

If you don't want to make the considerable investment in dollars and learning time that these products require, you should know that you can do at least eighty percent of what they're capable of doing by using either **Microsoft Word Version 5** or **Word Perfect 5.0** with a laser printer. In fact, many publishers now design and produce entire books using nothing but **Microsoft Word**.

Word Processors

The topic of word processors deserves its own book, so we'll keep the recommendations short. If you want a program you can grow with, the best choices are either **Microsoft Word** or **Word Perfect** in their latest iterations. Choosing between them is almost a toss-up with **Word** being favored if you're visually inclined and like working with a mouse. **WordPerfect** gets the nod if you like code-driven systems and don't like working with a mouse. Both programs are rock solid, their companies offer excellent technical support, and their apparently high price is easily offset by all the extra goodies they contain that you would otherwise have to buy separately.

If you're computer-phobic or want a program that doesn't require going through hundreds of pages to learn how to use, one of the best choices today is **Q&A Version 3** (Symantec). It can be learned in a few hours and combines a first-class word processor with one of the easiest-to-use data base managers available. It's ideal for people who don't spend a lot of time using a word processor and often need to retrieve information from files to put into the documents they do type. The word processor is also available separately as **Q & A Write**.

A Final Note

Two other coupons are included in the back of the book. You can use one to buy the diskette that's designed to accompany this book. You can use the other to buy another book-diskette combo we publish, **John C. Dvorak's PC Crash Course and Survival Guide**. It's a beginner's guide to the IBM-PC, and it can have you using a PC efficiently and confidently within a few hours.

Texts

Finally, here's a list of four books you should probably own if you sometimes feel as if you're married to your word processor. While none is presently available in machine-readable form, it probably won't be too long before they all are.

Brusaw, Charles T., Gerald J. Alred, and Walter E. Oliu. *Business Writer's Handbook*, 2nd edition. New York: St. Martin's Press, 1982.

> This handbook provides a comprehensive, practical reference guide to questions of grammar, punctuation, style, and usage. Arranged alphabetically, the book includes many examples.

Brusaw, Charles T., Gerald J. Alred, and Walter E. Oliu. *Handbook of Technical Writing*, 2nd edition. New York: St. Martin's Press, 1982.

> Similar to **Business Writer's Handbook**, this handbook also incorporates such topics as government proposals, graphs, specifications, and others specific to a technical writing environment. Arranged alphabetically, the book includes many examples.

Lanham, Richard J. *Revising Business Prose*. New York: Macmillan Publishing Company, 1987.

> This little book gives you a step-by-step analysis of how to hack your way through impenetrable prose and make it work.

Williams, Joseph M. *Style: Ten Lessons in Style and Grace*, 2nd edition. Glenview, Illinois: Scott, Foresman and Company, 1985.

> Of the many books on style, this book offers the most sophisticated approach. Master these ten lessons, and you will feel like a real master of your own prose.

Value Added I: Graphics Guide

Graphics Guide

SELECTING VISUAL FORMATS FOR DISPLAY OF DATA

Statistics may be presented graphically in many different ways, but there should always be a sound reason for choosing the particular form of presentation. There are only four basic types of charts—the line, bar chart, pie chart, and table—and one of them will be the right form for most statistical information you may want to display.

By and large, it is the material itself that will determine which kind is to be used, for it will naturally be visually clearer in that form than in any of the others. The purpose of making a graphic is to clarify or make visible the facts and message that otherwise would lie buried in a mass of written material, lists, balance sheets, or reports.

The type of graphic chosen must enlighten the reader/user/viewer. It should be seen as *the most obvious way* for the material to be shown.

This section will address six important questions about each one and will discuss and illustrate the differences:

1. What is the definition of graphic?
2. What are its main elements?
3. What variants are there?
4. What are appropriate uses?

5. What are inappropriate uses?

6. What are the main requirements/considerations?

Typical Curve

1. Definition

☐ Visualization of quantities, plotted over a time period, by means of using a rising/falling line

2. Main Elements

☐ Fever line, produced by joining together points plotted on a grid (otherwise known as "the curve")

☐ Y axis (vertical scale) represents quantities

☐ X axis (horizontal scale) represents time

3. Variants

☐ Single line, multiple line, three-dimensional line, combination with other types of graphics

4. Appropriate Uses

Unemployment figures, financial time series, stock indices, or any set of figures the flow of which needs to be shown over a period of time

5. Inappropriate Uses

☐ Information too close together statistically to distinguish among the lines

☐ Too little variation in quantities along a single line

6. Requirements/Considerations

☐ Easy to produce for a fast look at the flow of a set of figures

☐ Graph paper for initial plotting

☐ Colored pencils to distinguish lines of different figures

Typical Curve

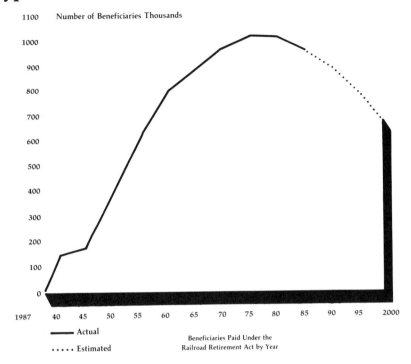

Number of Beneficiaries Thousands

—— Actual

••••• Estimated

Beneficiaries Paid Under the
Railroad Retirement Act by Year

Typical Bar Chart

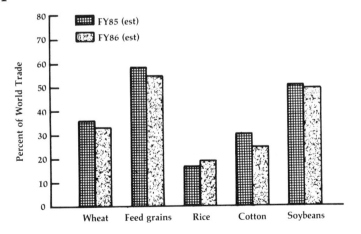

INTERNATIONALLY
U.S. Food/Agricultural Exports Account for a Major
Export Share of the World's Principal Crops

Typical Bar Chart

1. Definition

- ☐ Visualization of quantities, each one represented by an individual bar or column corresponding in height or length to the amount being counted

2. Main Elements

- ☐ Bars or elements grouped together in columns
- ☐ Grid or structural basis by which to understand the quantities

3. Variants

- ☐ Single row of abstract bars representing one commodity plotted over a time period
- ☐ Single row of abstract bars representing the values of different commodities all at the same time
- ☐ Bars as drawn representations of the commodity or subject described
- ☐ Multiple bars

4. Appropriate Uses

- ☐ Prominence given to individual figures rather than to overall flow
- ☐ comparison of different commodities; not a time series
- ☐ To complement and show a difference between two or more sets of figures charted over the same time period

5. Inappropriate Uses

- ☐ Too many numbers, which would make the bars too thin
- ☐ Where the flow is more important than the individual numbers

6. Requirements/Considerations

- ☐ Takes longer than fever chart
- ☐ Must be ruled out neatly to be convincing

Typical Table

1. Definition

☐ Display of numbers or words arranged in columns

2. Main Elements

☐ The series of numbers and their subject titles

☐ A grid/framework to contain them

3. Variants

☐ Simple columns, with or without illustrations

☐ An illustrated frame that describes subject matter

4. Appropriate Uses

☐ Timetables, flow charts, calendars, distance/mileage charts

☐ Comparisons of numbers that are too great in speed to be charted easily

☐ Where the exact numbers must be read, rather than illustrated as a generalized flow

5. Inappropriate Uses

☐ Where it is possible to plot the statistics as a chart

6. Requirements/Considerations

☐ Type is very important: It is the main element and must be readable

Payroll Tax Rates (1986-90)

(Percent of taxable wages and payroll)	1986	1987	1988	1989	1990
Social security:					
Employees	7.15	7.15	7.51	7.51	7.65
Employers	7.15	7.15	7.51	7.51	7.65
Total	14.30	14.30	15.02	15.02	15.30
Private pension					
Employees	4.25	4.25	4.25	4.25	4.25
Employers	14.75	14.75	14.75	14.75	14.75
Total	19.00	19.00	19.00	19.00	19.00

Typical Pie Chart

1. Definition

- ☐ The division of a whole into its components, usually in percentages

2. Main Elements

- ☐ Circle representing the complete number divided up by spokes from the center
- ☐ Segments formed as the radiating spokes touch the circumference of the circle, standing for the parts of the whole

3. Variants

- ☐ Flat, abstract two-dimensional
- ☐ Abstract three-dimensional
- ☐ As an element in an illustration or with illustrative elements attached to it

4. Appropriate Uses

- ☐ To show up to 8 or 10 component parts of a whole
- ☐ Budgets
- ☐ Share of market figures
- ☐ Analysis of income
- ☐ Income/spending

5. Inappropriate Uses

- ☐ Too many divisions, leading to impossibly small slices of the pie
- ☐ Too complicated an overall shape if it is not a circle

6. Requirements/Considerations

- ☐ Easily and quickly recognizable
- ☐ Can be used very small with great effect by color coding segments

Typical Pie Chart

Commodities Covered Under Price and Income Support Programs
Represent About Half of Total Cash Receipts

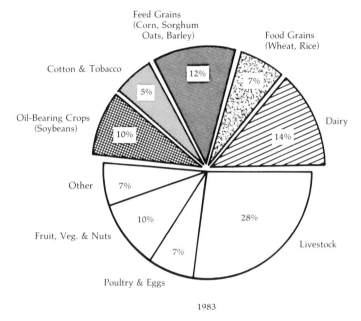

1983

Shaded slices are commodities covered by price and income support programs

---

Source: Connie Drake Wilson, Instructional Systems Consultant, Wilson Associates, Washington, D.C.

Value Added II: How to Lie with Statistics[1]

"The average Yaleman, Class of '24," *Time* magazine reported last year after reading something in the New York *Sun*, a newspaper published in those days, "makes $25,111 a year."

Well, good for him!

But, come to think of it, what does this improbably precise and salubrious figure mean? It is, as it appears to be, evidence that if you send your boy to Yale you won't have to work in your old age and neither will he? Is this average a mean or is it a median? What kind of sample is it based on? You could lump one Texas oilman with two hundred hungry free-lance writers and report *their* average income as $25,000-odd a year. The arithmetic is impeccable, the figure is convincingly precise, and the amount of meaning there is in it you could put in your eye.

In just such ways is the secret language of statistics, so appealing in a fact-minded culture, being used to sensationalize, inflate, confuse, and over simplify. Statistical terms are necessary in reporting the mass data of social and economic trends, business conditions, "opinion" polls, this year's census. But without writers who use the words with honesty and understanding and readers who know what they mean, the result can only be semantic nonsense.

---

[1]*HOW TO LIE WITH STATISTICS* By Darrell Huff. Reprinted from *How to Lie with Statistics* by Darrell Huff. Pictures by Irving Gels. By permission of W. W. Norton & Company, Inc. Copyright 1954 by Darrell Huff and Irving Gels.

In popular writing on scientific research, the abused statistic is almost crowding out the picture of the white-jacketed hero laboring overtime without time-and-a-half in an ill-lit laboratory. Like the "little dash of powder, little pot of paint," statistics are making an important fact "look like what she ain't." Here are some of the ways it is done.

The sample with the built-in bias. Our Yale men—or Yalemen, as they say in the Time-Life Building—belong to this flourishing group. The exaggerated estimate of their income is not based on all members of the class nor on a random or representative sample of them. At least two interesting categories of 1924-model Yale men have been excluded.

First there are those whose present addresses are unknown to their classmates. Wouldn't you bet that these lost sheep are earning less than the boys from prominent families and others who can be handily reached from a Wall Street office?

There are those who chucked the questionnaire into the nearest wastebasket. Maybe they didn't answer because they were not making enough money to brag about. Like the fellow who found a note clipped to his first pay check suggesting that he consider the salary amount confidential: "Don't worry," he told the boss. "I'm just as ashamed of it as you are."

Omitted from our sample then are just the two groups most likely to depress the average. The $25,111 figure is beginning to account for itself. It may indeed be a true figure for those of the Class of '24 whose addresses are known and who are willing to stand up and tell how much they earn. But even that requires a possibly dangerous assumption that the gentlemen are telling the truth.

To be dependable to any useful degree at all, a sampling study must use a representative sample (which can lead to trouble too) or a truly random one. If *all* the Class of '24 is included, that's all right. If every tenth name on a complete list is used, that is all right too, and so is drawing an adequate number of names out of a hat. The test is this: Does every name in the group have an equal chance to be in the sample?

You'll recall that ignoring this requirement was what produced the *Literary Digest's* famed fiasco.[2] When names for polling

---

[2]*Editor's note: The Literary Digest* predicted that Alfred Landon would defeat Franklin Roosevelt in the 1936 presidential election. Landon carried only two states.

were taken only from telephone books and subscription lists, people who did not have telephones or *Literary Digest* subscriptions had no chance to be in the sample. They possibly did not mind this underprivilege a bit, but their absence was in the end very hard on the magazine that relied on the figures.

This leads to a moral: You can prove about anything you want by letting your sample bias itself. As a consumer of statistical data—a reader, for example, of a news magazine—remember that no statistical conclusion can rise above the quality of the sample it is based upon. In the absence of information about the procedures behind it, you are not warranted in giving any credence at all to the result.

The truncated, or gee-whiz, graph. If you want to show some statistical information quickly and clearly, draw a picture of it. Graphic presentation is the thing today. If you don't mind misleading the hasty looker, or if you quite clearly *want* to deceive him, you can save some space by chopping the bottom off many kinds of graph.

Suppose you are showing the upward trend of national income month by month for a year. The total rise, as in one recent year, is 7 per cent. It looks like this:

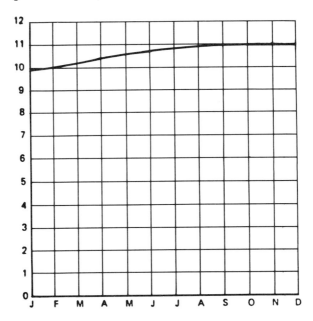

That is clear enough. Anybody can see that the trend is slightly upward. You are showing a 7 per cent increase and that is exactly what it looks like.

But it lacks schmaltz. So you chop off the bottom, this way:

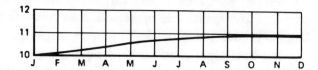

The figures are the same. It is the same graph and nothing has been falsified—except the impression that it gives. Anyone looking at it can just feel prosperity throbbing in the arteries of the country. It is a subtler equivalent of editing "National income rose 7 per cent" into ". . . climbed a whopping 7 per cent."

It is vastly more effective, however, because of that illusion of objectivity.

The souped-up graph. Sometimes truncating is not enough. The trifling rise in something or other still looks almost as insignificant as it is. You can make that 7 per cent look livelier than 100 per cent ordinarily does. Simply change the proportion between the ordinate and the abscissa. There's no rule against it, and it does give your graph a prettier shape.

But it exaggerates, to say the least, something awful:

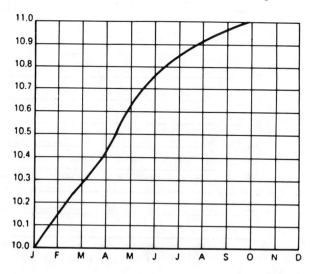

WRITING TO PLEASE YOUR BOSS

The well-chosen average. I live near a country neighborhood for which I can report an average income of $15,000. I could also report it as $3,500.

If I should want to sell real estate hereabouts to people having a high snobbery content, the first figure would be handy. The second figure, however, is the one to use in an argument against rising taxes, or the local bus fare.

Both are legitimate averages, legally arrived at. Yet it is obvious that at least one of them must be misleading as an out-and-out lie. The $15,000-figure is a mean, the arithmetic average of the incomes of all the families in the community. The smaller figure is a median; it might be called the income of the average family in the group. It indicates that half the families have less than $3,500 a year and half have more.

Here is where some of the confusion about averages comes from. Many human characteristics have the grace to fall into what is called the "normal" distribution. If you draw a picture of it, you get a curve that is shaped like a bell. Mean and median fall at about the same point, so it doesn't make very much difference which you use.

But some things refuse to follow this neat curve. Income is one of them. Incomes for most large areas will range from under $1,000 a year to upward of $50,000. Almost everybody will be under $10,000, way over on the left-hand side of that curve.

One of the things that made the income figure for the "average Yaleman" meaningless is that we are not told whether it is a mean or a median. It is not that one type of average is invariably better than the other; it depends upon what you are talking about. But neither gives you any real information—and either may be highly misleading—unless you know which of those two kinds of average it is.

In the country neighborhood I mentioned, almost everyone has less than the average—the mean, that is—of $10,500. These people are all small farmers, except for a trio of millionaire weekenders who bring up the mean enormously.

You can be pretty sure that when an income average is given in the form of a mean nearly everybody has less than that.

The insignificant difference or the elusive error. Your two children Peter and Linda (we might as well give them modish names while we're at it) take intelligence tests. Peter's IQ, you learn, is 98 and Linda's is 101. Aha! Linda is your brighter child.

Is she? An intelligence test is, or purports to be, a sampling of intellect. An IQ, like other products of sampling, is a figure with a statistical error, which expresses the precision or the reliability of the figure. The size of this probable error can be calculated. For their test the makers of the much-used Revised Stanford-Binet have found it to be about 3 per cent. So Peter's IQ of 98 really means only that there is an even chance that it falls between 95 and 101. There is an equal probability that it falls somewhere else—below 95 or above 101. Similarly, Linda's has no better than a fifty-fifty chance of being within the fairly sizeable range of 98 to 104.

You can work out the comparisons from that. One is that there is rather better than one chance in four that Peter, with his lower IQ rating, is really at least three points smarter than Linda. A statistician doesn't like to consider a difference significant unless you can hand him odds a lot longer than that.

Ignoring the error in a sampling study leads to all kinds of silly conclusions. There are magazine editors to whom readership surveys are gospel; with a 40 per cent readership reported for one article and a 35 per cent for another, they demand more like the first. I've seen even smaller differences given tremendous weight, because statistics are a mystery and numbers are impressive. The same thing goes for market surveys and so-called public opinion polls. The rule is that you cannot make a valid comparison between two such figures unless you know the deviations. And unless the difference between the figures is many times greater than the probable error of each, you have only a guess that the one appearing greater really is.

Otherwise you are like the man choosing a camp site from a report of mean temperature alone. One place in California with a mean annual temperature of 61 is San Nicolas Island on the south coast, where it always stays in the comfortable range between 47 and 87. Another with a mean of 61 is in the inland desert, where the thermometer hops around from 15 to 104. The deviation from the mean makes the difference, and you can freeze or roast if you ignore it.

The one-dimensional picture. Suppose you have just two or three figures to compare—say the average weekly wage of carpenters in the United States and another country. The sums might be $60 and $30. An ordinary bar chart makes the difference graphic.

That is an honest picture. It looks good for American carpenters, but perhaps it does not quite have the oomph you are after. Can't you make that difference appear overwhelming and at the same time give it what I am afraid is known as eye-appeal? Of course you can. Following tradition, you represent these sums by pictures of money bags. If the $30 bag is one inch high, you draw the $60 bag two inches high. That's in proportion, isn't it?

The catch is, of course, that the American's money bag, being twice as tall as that of the $30 man, covers an area on you page four times as great. And since your two-dimensional picture represents an object that would in fact have three dimensions, the money bags actually would differ much more than that. The volumes of any two similar solids vary as the cubes of their heights. If the unfortunate foreigner's bag holds $30 worth or dimes, the American's would hold not $60 but a neat $240.

You didn't say that, though, did you? And you can't be blamed, you're only doing it the way practically everybody else does.

The ever-impressive decimal. For a spurious air of precision that will lend all kinds of weight to the most disreputable statistics, consider the decimal.

Ask a hundred citizens how many hours they slept last night. Come out with a total of, say, 781.3. Your data was far from precise to begin with. Most people will miss their guess by fifteen minutes or more and some will recall five sleepless minutes as half a night of tossing insomnia.

But go ahead, do your arithmetic, announce that people sleep an average of 7.813 hours a night. You will sound as if you knew precisely what you are talking about. If you were foolish enough to say 7.8 (or "almost 8") hours it would sound like what it was—an approximation.

The semi-attached figure. If you can't prove what you want to prove, demonstrate something else and pretend that they are the same thing. In the daze that follows the collision of statistics with the human mind, hardly anybody will notice the difference. The semi-attached figure is a durable device guaranteed to stand you in good stead. It always has.

If you can't prove that your nostrum cures colds, publish a sworn laboratory report that the stuff killed 31,108 germs in a test tube in eleven seconds. There may be no connection at all between assorted germs in a test tube and the whatever-it-is that produces colds, but people aren't going to reason that sharply, especially while sniffling.

Maybe that one is too obvious and people are going to catch on. Here is a trickier version.

Let us say that in a period where race prejudice is growing it is to your advantage to "prove" otherwise. You will not find it a difficult assignment.

Ask that usual cross section of the population if they think Negroes have as good a chance as white people to get jobs. Ask again a few months later. As Princeton's Office of Public Opinion Research has found out, people who are most unsympathetic to Negroes are the ones most likely to answer yes to this question.

As prejudice increases in a country, the percentage of affirmative answers you will get to this question becomes larger. What looks on the face of it like growing opportunity for Negroes is actually mounting prejudice and nothing else. You have achieved something rather remarkable: the worse things get, the better the survey makes them look.

The unwarranted assumption, or post hoc *rides again.* The interrelation of cause and effect, so often obscure anyway, can be neatly hidden in statistical data.

Somebody once went to a good deal of trouble to find out if cigarette smokers make lower college grades than non-smokers. They did. This naturally pleased many people, and they made much of it.

The unwarranted assumption, of course, was that smoking had produced dull minds. It seemed vaguely reasonable on the face of it, so it was quite widely accepted. But it really proved nothing of the sort, any more than it proved that poor grades drive students to the solace of tobacco. Maybe the relationship worked in one direction, maybe in the other. And maybe all this is only an indication that the sociable sort of fellow who is likely to take his books less than seriously is also likely to sit around and smoke many cigarettes.

Permitting statistical treatment to befog causal relationships is little better than superstition. It is like the conviction among the people of the Hebrides that body lice produce good health. Observation over the centuries had taught them that people in good health had lice and sick people did not. *Ergo,* lice made a man healthy. Everybody should have them.

Scantier evidence, treated statistically at the expense of common sense, has made many a medical fortune and many a medical article in magazines, including professional ones. More sophisticated observers finally got things straightened out in the Hebrides. As it turned out, almost everybody in those circles had lice most of the time. But when a man took a fever (quite possibly carried to him by those same lice) and his body became hot, the lice left.

Here you have cause and effect not only reversed, but intermingled.

There you have a primer in some ways to use statistics to deceive. A well-wrapped statistic is better than Hitler's "big lie": it misleads, yet it can't be pinned onto you.

Is this little list altogether too much like a manual for swindlers? Perhaps I can justify it in the manner of the retired burglar whose published reminiscences amounted to a graduate course in how to pick a lock and muffle a footfall: The crooks already know these tricks. Honest men must learn them in self-defense.

Value Added III: Worksheets and Checklists

Decision 1
Worksheet

Instructions: Write an answer to each question.

Statement of the Problem

Why do I need to do this job? What is at issue?

Technical Purpose

What do I need to do in order to know what I need to know?

Communication Purpose

What does my document need to do? What do I need to say in order for someone else to know?

Decision 2
Worksheet A

Instructions: List all of your readers under Users and Reviewers.
Then fill in the chart for each reader.

	Need for Document	Knowledge of My Task	Level of Expertise	Mastery of Relevant Vocabulary
Users				
Reviewers				

Decision 2
Worksheet B

Instructions: Decide who is the most important reader for your document. Answer the following questions for that reader.

Key reader: _____

Role within the
organization: _____

_____

Why this reader
needs my document: _____

_____

_____

Reader's knowledge
of my task: _____

_____

Reader's knowledge
of technical area: _____

_____

Reader's education
and professional
experience: _____

_____

_____

Reader's attitudes
that might bear on
my document: _____

_____

Decision 3
Worksheet

Instructions: List your readers in the left-hand column, and for each one list the assumptions you can make about what the reader knows. In the right-hand column, list the questions about the subject that each reader is likely to have.

Readers	Assumptions (what the reader already knows)	Questions (what you need to tell the reader)
1. _____	_____	_____
	_____	_____
	_____	_____
	_____	_____
	_____	_____
	_____	_____
	_____	_____
2. _____	_____	_____
	_____	_____
	_____	_____
	_____	_____
	_____	_____
	_____	_____

Decision 4 Worksheet

Instructions: In the left-hand column, fill in your anticipated readers. Then describe what role you can appropriately play in relation to that reader.

Readers   Writer's Role in Relation to Reader

_____   _____

                                 _____

                                 _____

_____   _____

                                 _____

                                 _____

_____   _____

                                 _____

                                 _____

_____   _____

                                 _____

                                 _____

_____   _____

                                 _____

Decision 5
Worksheet

Instructions: Go through your research notes or working papers and mark all the items of information you might conceivably use in your document. Write each item of information on an individual Post-it ™ note (the kind that sticks on paper, but can be removed and placed elsewhere). Don't censor yourself or edit the notes; your object at this stage is simply to generate a stockpile. When you have made a stockpile, assemble the Post-it ™ notes in storyboard fashion. You will find it helpful to spread them out on a large sheet of paper (flip-chart size). It can be rolled and stored for further work, it can be moved easily, and it can be hung on the wall.

Decision 6
Worksheet

Instructions: Work with your storyboard. Examine your first groupings of Post-it ™ notes to see whether your preliminary categories are viable. Look for exceptionally large bodies of data under one category—a sign that the category needs to be divided. Also look for relevance of facts to each other within a category. If some seem not to belong together, put them in a different category. Regroup until two things seem possible:

1. all facts within a category can be arranged in a meaningful order, and
2. all categories can be arranged in a meaningful order.

Decision 7
Worksheet

Instructions: Use 3" × 5" Post-it ™ notes for this stage of your storyboard. Write each of your topic headings on a 3" × 5" Post-it ™ note. Look at each topic and see what answers it suggests to your reader's questions about the subject. (See Decision 3.) Expand the topic into a complete statement that answers the questions, then arrange the statements in order. Use the order of your topic outline first. To see if the statements make sense in that order, read them aloud. They should tell the "story" you are trying to convey. If they don't make sense in that order, try changing the order or the statements themselves.

In moving from topics to statements, you should be able to accomplish two things:

1. say what you mean *about* each of your topics, and
2. arrange the points in order. (You may find at this stage that the order of your categories needs to change.)

Decision 8
Worksheet

Instructions: Add the following elements to your statement outline: an executive summary (or abstract or digest) and an introductory paragraph for each section. You already have captions and topic sentences from the statement outline in Decision 7.

Collaborating
Worksheet

1. Do I share my statement of purpose with my supervisor?

2. Do I share my statement outline with my supervisor?

3. Can I share informal planning decisions with my supervisor? If not, with whom can I verify these decisions?

4. What managerial style does my current manager have?

   ☐ "I'll know what I want when I see it."

   ☐ "If I want it to turn out right, I'll have to do it myself."

   ☐ "It should be right the first time—it shouldn't need any changes."

   ☐ "If I could figure it out when I was new, they can figure it out too."

5. What can I do to cope with my manager's style?

Decision 9
Worksheet

1. Do I need quiet or some distraction to write my best?

2. What is the best place for me to draft?

3. What is the best time of day for me to draft?

4. What changes in my schedule do I need to make in order to be able to draft during my best time?

5. I would rather draft with one of the following:

   ☐ word processor or personal computer
   ☐ lined paper
   ☐ unlined paper
   ☐ pencil
   ☐ pen
   ☐ other

6. How do I get what I need to draft?

7. What "essentials" do I need to make me comfortable when drafting (coffee, cookies, chips, fruit, whatever)?

8. Can I remember that a first draft is a rough draft and doesn't have to be perfect?

Decision 10
Worksheet

1. Do I review my planning documents before I draft?

2. How often do I seem to need a break from drafting? Do I take it?

3. Do I plan my drafting schedule for ninety-minute segments?

Decision 11
Worksheet A: Finding Graphics

Instructions: Answer the following questions. Any question to which you answer "yes" is a potential graphic for your report.

Subject

Do I have a physical object that I could show?

Am I comparing one total with other totals?

Am I showing the relative importance of elements as components of a whole?

Am I showing the frequency of distribution over time or in a location?

Am I showing change over a period of time?

Am I showing the relative values of a variety of elements?

Am I indicating a complex process?

Am I including detailed information that I could put into a matrix for reference?

Do I have an important point that I could emphasize visually?

Source: Connie Drake Wilson, Instructional Systems Consultant, Wilson Associates, Washington, D.C.

Decision 11
Worksheet B: Planning Graphics

Instructions: Answer the following questions for each visual aid you are considering.

Purpose
What is the point that I want to make with this visual aid? What's the message that I'm trying to convey?

Audience
Who is the audience for this visual aid?

Is the type of graphic familiar to them?

Is the design simple?

Where do I need to include "cue" words for the audience?

How can I make the graphic efficient for the audience to read?

Decision 12
Worksheet

To check for advance organizers, capitalize on the outline you worked on in Decisions 5 through 8.

1. Do my major points in the outline occupy positions of major visibility?
2. Have I provided an executive summary, if possible?
3. Does my title indicate the major theme of my report?
4. Have I used headings and subheadings to mark major sections of the report?
5. Have I used summary statements as overviews to forecast information for my reader?
6. Have I used topic sentences to guide my reader through a paragraph?
7. Have I used guide words or transitions to help a reader predict the points of my document?
8. Have I used typographic arrangement to emphasize my main points?
9. Have I used highlighting techniques to emphasize my points?
10. Have I overused typographic arrangement or highlighting techniques?
11. Have I used graphics to emphasize important points?

Decision 13
Worksheet

Instructions: Answer the following questions for a draft of your own document.

1. What is my communication purpose?
2. What theme or message emerges when I read the topic sentences of the document?
3. Have I grouped similar information within a paragraph?
4. Have I used transitions to guide my reader through the logic of a paragraph?

Decision 14
Worksheet

Use a sample of your own professional writing.
1. Skim down the margin looking for the extra white spaces that mark the ends of sentences.
2. Mark any place that has very long (about three lines) or very short (about half a line) sentences.
3. Check that the content of the short sentences is appropriate to receive the emphasis the short sentence naturally provides.
4. Count the words in the long sentences and check where they fall on the Readability chart above.
5. Graph the lengths, if you wish.
6. Decide whether you need to shorten or lengthen sentences.
7. Examine all actions to determine where your sentence core should be.
8. Look for possible frozen action, words ending in "ion," "ness," "ity," or "ance."

Decision 14
Worksheet B

Directions: Choose a selection from a final product that you have recently produced. Graph your sentence lengths to find what seems to be your natural "revised" length.

Choose another selection from a draft of a product that you have recently written. Graph these sentence lengths to find what seems to be your natural "drafting" length.

STRUCTURED READING FOR REVIEWERS

Advance Organizers

Is an executive summary provided?

Does the title indicate the major theme of the report? Do the headings and subheadings mark major sections of the report?

Are summary statements used as overviews to forecast information for my reader?

Do the topic sentences tell the story of the document?

Does the typographic arrangement emphasize the main points? Are highlighting techniques used to emphasize main points? Are typographic arrangement or highlighting techniques overused?

Do graphics emphasize important points?

Paragraphs

Do clusters of paragraphs or sections provide a unified context? Is the order logical?

Do individual paragraphs support the topic sentence?

Do guide words or transitions help the reader predict the points of the document?

Sentences

Are any sentences too long or too short?

Do sentences place important information in the sentence core?

Are sentences concise and precise?

Words and Phrases

Are words and phrases used grammatically and idiomatically?

Is jargon a problem in the document?

Are there spelling or punctuation errors?

Manager's Checklist For Writing Problems

What is the general writing problem?

- ☐ Does the message lack clear analysis?
- ☐ Does the presentation lack clear structure?
- ☐ Is the language inappropriate?
- ☐ Is the English incorrect?

What is the specific writing problem?

- ☐ Does the document fail to fulfill its purpose?
- ☐ Are the reader's needs not generally met?
- ☐ Is the subject treated too narrowly or broadly?
- ☐ Is the writer's stance inappropriate?
- ☐ Are the facts inaccurate?
- ☐ Is the data irrelevant?
- ☐ Are the theoretical assumptions invalid?
- ☐ Is the reasoning inappropriate to the purpose of the document?
- ☐ Is the document organized without a clear, apparent structure?
- ☐ Has the writer failed to use headings to increase the accessibility of the message?
- ☐ Has the writer failed to use topic sentences to open paragraphs?
- ☐ Has the writer failed to arrange points in a logical progression?
- ☐ Are the sentences too long or too short?
- ☐ Are the sentences illogical?
- ☐ Does the writer use inappropriate terms?
- ☐ Does the writer use jargon?
- ☐ Is the grammar incorrect?
- ☐ Are spelling and punctuation incorrect?
- ☐ Is the language not idiomatic?

How much does the problem matter?

- ☐ Can I solve it by simple editing?
- ☐ Does solving the problem require redrafting the document?
- ☐ Does solving the problem require that I redraft the document myself?

What is the source of the problem?

- ☐ Does the writer lack skill in English?
- ☐ Does the writer lack composition skills?
- ☐ Does the writer lack sufficient technical expertise for the topic of the report?
- ☐ Does the writer lack experience in this type of document?
- ☐ Did I fail to give the writer enough information about the assignment?
- ☐ Is the assignment complex?

What will solve the writer's problem?

- ☐ Training in English as a Second Language?
- ☐ Review of the basics of English grammar?
- ☐ Training in written communication?
- ☐ Further research or education?
- ☐ Giving the writer models of this type of document?
- ☐ Explaining my expectations in greater detail?
- ☐ Monitoring the progress of the assignment to help shape the thought process?

Demo Copy
Resale Prohibited

Demo Copy
Resale Prohibited